S. JAMES MEYER

# The Whole in our Soul

Reconciliation with ***Everything***

TWENTY-THIRD PUBLICATIONS
twentythirdpublications.com

*In deep gratitude for the generous man from Minnesota whom I will never meet, the guy who donated his cornea to me, a total stranger, so that I might see and marvel and write. I could not have written this book without his gift. He now lives in me, and I live through him. I believe that's how God intended things.*

*Thank you, Sir.*

**TWENTY-THIRD PUBLICATIONS**
977 Hartford Turnpike Unit A, Waterford, CT 06385
(860) 437-3012 or (800) 321-0411 • twentythirdpublications.com



Cover photo: sompong / stock.adobe.com • ISBN: 978-1-62785-879-3
Printed in the U.S.A.

# CONTENTS

# INTRODUCTION

I was a happy accident. Mostly. My parents already had two children under the age of two. Welcoming and supporting a third on an inexperienced carpenter's wages, well, let's just say I wasn't in the plan. Who is kidding who, though? It was the early 1960s in rural Wisconsin. People didn't make such plans. As my mother would tell me many years later, "We didn't make plans. We made do."

It was a simpler time and place, a world in which people knew their neighbors and looked out for one another. Mostly. However, I don't want to romanticize the past in a way that negates the institutionalized racism, sexism, abuse, and other pains of that era. A lot of people suffered, and a lot of people were perfectly content to advance and profit from systems that enabled suffering. Still, I came of age in a culture that knew something was amiss. There was an undercurrent of belief that all people are sacred and should be treated with dignity, and even though this belief was often compromised, there was a social conscience of sorts telling us that we shouldn't be comfortable with such transgressions. We should try to be better.

Here's the thing I can't get past: over sixty years later, we still have racism, sexism, abuse, and so many other pains, but we don't know that something is amiss, and we don't know our neighbors nearly as well, nor do we look out for them nearly as much. I'm not talking, of course, about the neighbors living to the left and right of us. I'm talking about the neighbors who stock our grocery shelves, work in our clinics and hospitals, and harvest our crops. I'm talking about our neighbors as Jesus meant when he told us to love our neighbors as ourselves.

Instead of growing closer and deeper over the last several generations, we have grown increasingly estranged. Instead of planting and nurturing seeds of love, we are sowing and growing seeds of division and even hatred. We have grown so far apart that in almost all walks of life, our public conversation is consumed by animosity, antagonism, and fear. None of us would choose to live this way, yet we do choose to live this way every day, which means we are even divided within our own selves.

I fear we fight with each other because we don't know what else to do with all our angst. We are broken, living with the stress of fracture within ourselves, our relationships, our churches, our communities, our country, and our world. Indeed, we have become so mired in division that we can no longer even imagine a way out. So, we argue and fight some more, like children stuck in the back seat of the car, except there are no parents threatening to pull the car over and make us walk.

I offer this book as a path forward, a way out. But it's not new thinking. In fact, it is ancient. It is the same path forward that the sandal-strapped Nazorean lived and died for two thousand years ago. It is the path to wholeness. This book brings it into the contemporary context where we can apply it in our lives and, hopefully, not ignore or dismiss it as old and irrelevant.

In attempting to illustrate how the idea of reconciliation is the on-ramp to wholeness, I did not intend to reconcile the odd and ironic division between spirituality and religion. Yet, as you read you may experience that reconciliation unfolding on its own. People often ask me if my books are more spiritual or more religious. It's a head-scratching inquiry because I think we all agree religion and spirituality should not be two separate things. We want them to be fused, as they should be.

Nonetheless, if cornered and forced to answer the question about whether this particular book is more spiritual or religious, I will say, "Yes."

Happy accident.

part one

# Choosing Reconciliation over Resolution

1

# Leaving Brokenness, Restoring Wholeness

My dad loved cars. He was gobsmacked by the engineering, styling, mechanics, power, all of it. He loved the way a well-tuned engine came alive like an orchestra when he pressed the accelerator, as though he was God breathing life into clay. Mostly, he loved the freedom cars provided. For a boy who grew up on a dairy farm outside a rural hamlet aptly named Loyal, an automobile represented liberty. Four wheels powered by eight cylinders could take him anywhere to see anything, all on his own terms and under his own control.

I share this to help you understand the magnitude of the story that follows. It is not enough to say my father loved cars. He saw them as instruments of possibility and metaphors for self-actualization. In the final weeks of his life, knowing he was at the end of his road, his last act on this earth was to purchase a brand new, highly reliable vehicle my mother could count on to live freely after he was gone. In Dad's frame of reference, a car was not merely a tool of conveyance; it was an extension of self and an expression of love.

## The Brougham

In 1978, Dad threw pragmatism to the wind and purchased a new Mercury Marquis Brougham. This black-tie specimen was about forty-eight feet long, had an engine the size of a bulldozer, and was appointed with every conceivable luxury of the era, right down to overly designed retractable headlight covers that raised and lowered like eyelids. It was space-age. The neighbor kids thought my dad had purchased a limousine. They had never seen such a car except on television.

As much as Dad loved that car, he also loved his son, so he assigned me the privilege (his word) of hand washing and waxing it—a task that would consume an entire day, if done properly. I remember thinking there was something incarnate about the whole thing, that I, his son, should be sent to toil for my father's glory. But there were moments when it was my glory, too. At sixteen, I took my driver's test in that car. As the examiner settled into the passenger's seat, he rolled his head in all directions, assessing the full acreage of the machine, and then he released a long, slow, audible breath before saying, "I don't think I'll be asking you to parallel park." God bless him.

On rare occasions, usually when one of my sisters was using our family's other vehicle, I was allowed to take the "hearse" (a nickname assigned by my friends) to work or elsewhere. This, I fully understood, was an act of trust and confidence. Given the driving skill required to maneuver such an impressive wheelbase into and out of parking stalls, it was one of the few things during my teen years that gave me the satisfaction of knowing that my father truly believed in me.

## The Dark Night

In the wee hours one late summer Saturday, I pulled into the driveway with my dad's car shortly after two in the morning. I had worked until ten o'clock Friday night, so if you're wondering what on earth I was doing for four hours, please allow me the benefit of your doubt. I'll offer two equally likely options to assuage your curiosity: 1) I had stopped on my way home to fill the car with gas, and the extremely large tank took nearly four hours to top off; or 2) I had stopped at one of those 24/7 perpetual adoration chapels and fell asleep. If there was a third option involving a Spanish exchange student named Elaina, I see no point in chasing it from all these decades hence.

Given the curvature of my parents' driveway, the narrowness of the garage door, and the size of the car, it was easier to back into the garage than to back out. As I was reversing this boat into its slip, my breath was halted by the sickening sound of metal grinding against wood. My stomach knotted. I jumped out and assessed the damage: white paint on the driver's side front fender, black paint on the white door jam. Instinctively, I grabbed the Turtle Wax to buff out the scratches or at least minimize the damage, but the effort was mostly futile. Alas, I had done more than scrape the fender. I had dented it.

There comes a defining moment in every life when we must walk up the stairs and take responsibility for our decisions and actions, when we must come face to face with truth and see how we measure up. For Luke Skywalker, that moment came in a cave on Dagobah. For Jesus the Nazorean, it came when facing temptations in the desert. For me, that moment would come in a driveway on East Ninth Street, but it could wait until morning. I went to bed.

## Reckoning

Shortly after seven, I awoke and looked out the window to see my father standing in the driveway. The garage door was up. His hands were on his hips. He stared at his car for a long time, then turned his head to look at the doorjamb. Then back to the car. His fingers reached out and gently touched the wound. I swallowed, realizing I had best get out there and face my truth.

The men in my mother's family are not tall. The men in my father's family are. I inherited the height of my maternal clan, so as I approached my father that morning, he stood a good three inches over me even as he drooped in sadness. He was a man of impressive stature: strong, with calloused hands. He drank his coffee black and read *Popular Mechanics*; I drank Mountain Dew and read John Steinbeck. He wore Red Wing work boots; I wore flipflops. We had nothing in common. Except flesh and blood.

The all-too-familiar feeling of having once again disappointed my father collapsed my ribcage against my lungs. But I had learned how much he respected people who stood up and took responsibility, people who didn't hide behind excuses or attempt to BS their way out of their own mistakes and bad decisions. Honesty and humility were the two yardsticks by which he measured a man, so full confession and contrition provided my only hope of redemption.

The words sincerely spilled from my mouth as I stepped toward him. "Dad, I am so very sorry. I feel terri..."

His hand went up, silently cutting me off. We looked at each other across nineteen years of equal parts love and frustration. Then he spoke. "Here's what's going to happen, Steve. One day you'll have a son who wrecks one of your cars. I want you to treat him exactly the way I am treating you. Now, let's go have breakfast."

He never mentioned it again. Not once. Not ever.

## What Could Have Been

In the darkness of adversity, my father showed me the depth of his character. There are many other ways he could have responded, many ways that would have been more expected and more common perhaps. He could have yelled and screamed. He could have insulted, diminished, and belittled me. He could have pounded his fist and stomped his foot, leveling consequences and punishments. Instead, he chose mercy, kindness, and forgiveness. He chose to prioritize his love for his son over his love for his car. Think about that. He made our relationship more valuable than the object. Why is that so surprising to so many of us?

Here's the thing, though—any other response would have amplified the brokenness. My father's chosen response restored wholeness.

I'll unpack that in a moment, but first allow me to address the single biggest question I get when I share this story while speaking to groups: What about accountability? Should my father have levied consequences to hold me accountable, such as requiring me to pay to repair the car and/or refusing to allow me to drive any of his vehicles until I worked off the debt? Where was the penance?

## The Accountability Issue

We can dismiss the question of accountability. It wasn't necessary. I owned the mishap. I held myself accountable, so why would my father have to? The obvious evidence being that I stepped forward with an admission and apology at the first opportunity. In raising my own sons, I sought to teach them that spiritually mature people own their own stuff, except I likely used a less polite s-word than "stuff." Let's pretend I used the word "shadow." Spiritually mature people own their own shadow, referring collectively to mistakes, omissions, addictions, prejudices, transgressions, and darknesses of all varieties. Basically, everything and anything we would prefer to hide from the light.

The less obvious (but equally critical) evidence that I held myself accountable was that I made no attempt to blame anything else. I did not complain that the garage door was too narrow, the driveway too curvy, the car too big, or the night too dark. My father had no need to hold me accountable because I, and I alone, accepted full responsibility through my own fault, through my most grievous fault.

## The Consequence Issue

Among any group of listeners, a few will respond to this story by suggesting my dad should have imposed some sort of financial consequence, that a good father would teach his son that justice demands retribution. I understand the human appeal of this argument, but let's be honest about the financial power dynamic at play. I was a nineteen-year-old college kid. While my parents were by no means wealthy, they were certainly in a more stable financial position than I was. I would have been forced to drop out of school for a semester to pay such a debt. While that might seem fair to some, I was blessed to have a father who saw things differently. The human cost of the consequence would have outweighed the financial cost of the error. Besides, my dad had a much more valuable lesson to teach me.

To be clear, my father did levy a consequence. He instructed me to treat my own son with the same forgiveness and mercy he was showing me. In that moment, he taught me that the price of being forgiven is to pay it forward. This idea is so ingrained in Christian prayer that we speak it from memory without even thinking about what it means: *forgive us our trespasses as we forgive those who trespass against us*. Perhaps we should slow down and think about what we're saying.

For justice to happen, consequences do not necessarily have to come in the form of payback; they can come in the form of pay forward. In fact, this is the preferred method among spiritual people because it amplifies mercy rather than emphasizing retribution. In a very real sense, my father turned the other cheek. Instead of looking back at the damage I had done, he turned and looked forward toward the potential good that could come out of it. If "paschal mystery" were to be used as a verb, it would describe what he did. He *paschal-mysteried* this thing, transforming sorrow to joy and death to life.

## Teaching Mercy

Those who raise questions about accountability and consequence often do so with the judgy overtone of defensiveness. They subtly suggest that perhaps my father was a negligent parent for not "teaching me a lesson" and for "letting me get away with it." Hmm.

Setting aside the insinuation that my father's act of mercy was an abandonment of his parental duty and his son (me) turned out to be some sort of amoral social miscreant as a result, let me pose this question: Why do we think it is more important to emphasize retribution than mercy? Why do we think a lesson in the tough love of punishment is more responsible than a lesson about the unconditional love of forgiveness? And why do we as adults buy into the schoolyard logic that vengeance shows strength, and forgiveness shows weakness, when we know deep in our souls that letting something go often takes a thousand times more strength than clinging to it? It took a lot more emotional and spiritual fortitude for my dad to simply tell me to pay it forward and then never mention his damaged car again than it would have to blow a gasket and diminish me for making a costly error.

Why is it that we would rather resolve our suffering by paying pain forward than reconcile it by paying mercy forward? Our prisons, homeless shelters, and therapy offices are overflowing with suffering souls who have been caught in generational cycles of unrequited abuse that has been paid forward, each generation passing its pain to the next. If we can't get revenge upon the person who hurt us, we balance the scales by hurting someone else or even hurting ourselves or our own children. The Center for Action and

Contemplation teaches that those who don't transform their pain will transfer their pain. Blame and retribution transfer; mercy and forgiveness transform. Blessed are the merciful, indeed. For mercy shall be theirs.

## Resolution vs. Reconciliation

Earlier, I mentioned that any other response from my father would have amplified brokenness. While it might have assuaged his anger and felt justified for a moment, any other approach would not have improved the situation. Also, it would have left me feeling even more broken than the car. He chose instead to restore wholeness. This is the foundational difference between resolution and reconciliation. Although it is seldom discussed, it is something we desperately need to understand.

When faced with conflict or stress, our egos typically seek to resolve our negative emotions by lashing back at the perceived source of the conflict. This sort of tit-for-tat retributive justice feels like resolution, but it resolves nothing. Instead, it is a counterproductive waste of energy that empowers resentment, fear, and other dark emotions. It further divides us rather than unifying us.

If, for example, you say something hurtful to me, I feel justified in resolving my broken feelings by saying something hurtful to you. If you strike me, I'll strike you. If you sin against me, I'll sin against you. On the surface, this may feel like I'm taking my power back—but it's not real power, it's merely ego power, like the sound chip in a child's toy—and then I immediately use that illusion of power to put more animosity, hurtfulness, and negativity into the world. I haven't really resolved the situation at all: I've only resolved my feelings about the situation, and in doing so I've amplified the brokenness.

Regardless of anyone's religious beliefs about Jesus, the man was a brilliant ethicist and moral philosopher. He replaced eye-for-an-eye justice with turn-the-other-cheek justice; he gave us the idea of paying forgiveness forward; and he rewrote the rules by saying that if someone takes your coat, you should give them your shirt as well. Under the small and narrow scope of our human reasoning, this strikes us as allowing darkness to win the day, so we relegate it to the fringes of faith, or we ignore it altogether. Some among us, even some devout Christians who wear Jesus on their sleeves, go so far as to consider this to be a sign of weakness. But this sandal-wearing sage from Nazareth understood something the rest of us have yet to learn: retribution only serves to double down on the darkness. It makes the world worse instead of better.

If you are wondering why there is so much anger, brokenness, and suffering in the world, ask yourself if it's because we keep choosing to resolve conflicts in our own way rather than reconciling them in the way Christ encouraged us. We respond to darkness and brokenness by putting more darkness and brokenness into the world. It's not working. We need to fight fire with water, not with an even hotter fire; and we need to confront hatred with love, not with an even hotter hatred.

## Full Circle

I was working in my study late on a Saturday afternoon when one of my teenage sons stepped through the door and softly said, "Dad, you'd better come outside." This particular young man was notorious for shenanigans, and my first instinct was to make sure I wasn't walking into a water gun assault, so I looked at him a little side-eyed. But he also seldom spoke softly, so I decided to take him seriously.

When I reached the driveway, I saw that he had backed my truck out of the garage and had scraped it along the entire length of another car parked in the driveway. He had taken out two of my vehicles in one swipe! I hung my head and took a deep breath.

"Dad," he started. "I am so, so very sor..."

My hand went up. "Stop," I said. I reached over, put my arm around him, and held him close. "Here's what's going to happen. One day, one of my grandchildren who I love very much is going to ruin one of your cars. I want you to treat him exactly the same way I am treating you. Now, let's go get some ice cream."

It took thirty years, but justice had been served. My father had been justified. Mercy is a gift that pays forward.

2

# Choosing a Third Way in a Two-Way World

A brilliant little story in the Gospel of John (8:1–11) captures the social and political landscape of ancient Jerusalem. It portrays a dynamic surprisingly like the social and political landscape we live in today, even though we like to pretend Jesus' context was different from ours. In the light of today's world, the gospel can be a little inconvenient and unsettling. Sometimes it's easier to hide behind the notion that many of Christ's teachings were tethered to a long-ago culture and don't really apply to us and the world in which we live today. Love your neighbor? Love your enemy? Blessed are the poor? Yikes! Is he kidding?! In reality, we haven't changed nearly as much as we think we have in two millennia.

Before we get into it, let's all pause and take a deep breath, OK? Seriously. Maybe even take a slow walk in fresh air and reconnect with both Creator and creation. As soon as many of us see or hear the words "social" and "political," we brace for impact. We've been conditioned like Pavlovian dogs to bristle and recoil at the mere mention of the terms "socially" and "politically," as though everything we hold sacred is about to be attacked. That's a problem. Arguably, our need to be right about everything is a false god, a violation of Commandment Number One on the Top Ten list.

Even as you read this, many are hoping that what follows will validate their existing social and political leanings. And if the ensuing discussion does not align, they will activate a fight and/or flight response, slamming the book closed and cursing my ancestors. This is how Jesus ended up on a cross, you know. He didn't pledge allegiance to the prevailing structures of power. He didn't really challenge them either, other than turning over a few tables in the temple area, but he didn't validate the man-made social and economic system. He simply pointed out that there's a better way, and that alone made him a threat. Again, I'm not sure we've changed a whole lot. But I believe him; there's a better way.

## The Trap

A group of hand-wringing Scribes and Pharisees brought forth a woman caught in the very act of adultery. Thankfully, the story offers no sordid details about how exactly the sting went down, but there was no question of her guilt. They were ready to move directly to sentencing. No need for a trial. No need to let her confront her accuser. No acknowledgment whatsoever of her human rights or dignity as a person created in God's image. No mention of the guy she was involved with. She broke the law and needed to be held accountable.

It was the perfect set-up for their agenda. Finally, they had an airtight case with which to pin Jesus down. Either he would affirm the law and agree the woman should be stoned, or he would lean heavily into his thematic message about love and mercy, thereby rendering the law irrelevant and effectively placing his own judgment above the law. Keep in mind that this wasn't about civic law, it was about God's law.

Let's look at the logic. The Pharisees gave Jesus two options. That's it, only two. The first option—Choice A, stone her—represents what we today would call orthodox, traditional, or conservative. It draws a hard line between right and wrong. Some would defend it as an adherence to the social order and respect for the rule of law. Others would critique it as inhumane, cruel, and absolutist. The second option—Choice B, let her go—represents the position which contemporary parlance would label as progressive, reformist, or liberal. It suggests that life is ambiguous and there are a lot of gray areas. Some would defend it as an acknowledgment of realism and respect for individual circumstances. Others would critique it as wishy-washy, morally arbitrary, and permissive.

As far as the Scribes and Pharisees were concerned, one of these choices was clearly right, and one was clearly wrong. If Jesus goes with Choice A, no problem, but he will have publicly acknowledged that law takes priority over mercy. If he takes Choice B, big problem. Huge. He will be placing his teaching about mercy over God's law. Either way, they got him! Finally, they got him!

## The Pause

Before Jesus says anything, he bends down and draws in the dirt with his finger. It's an often-overlooked detail, but a genius strategic move toward reconciling the conflict. This simple action achieves and teaches three things we can all learn about dealing with disagreements and paradoxes.

First, it buys time and introduces an aura of quiet. It's a deep breath with which to calm the storm. Much research has been done recently on the difference between fast and slow thinking, between surface level and deep thinking. The Scribes and Pharisees have everyone stirred up in a tempest of surface-level, emotionally charged thought, and Jesus wants to slow the mindset down so deep, meaningful, spiritually engaged discernment can happen. A common term for this moment of silence would be meditation or prayer, and it is essential if we want to transform conflict and animosity into unity and wholeness. That's a big *if*, isn't it? We will never have peace in our own hearts or on our planet as long as we prefer conflict over unity and animosity over wholeness.

Second, by drawing in the dirt, he shifts the focus. All eyes had been fixed on the adulterous woman, on him, and on the conflict. What's going to happen to her? What's he going to say? Human nature being what it is, we can reasonably assume that about half the people wanted him to condemn the woman, and half wanted him to forgive her. Half tilted toward an orthodox or conservative approach, and half toward a progressive or liberal approach. To help clear heads, Jesus shifts attention to something he doodles in the dirt, giving everyone a common focus apart from the conflict at hand. The story doesn't tell us what he wrote or drew, an omission that suggests the image is not important, but the action is. When seeking to reconcile conflicts in our own lives, we are wise to likewise clear our heads and shift our focus away from the singular perspective on which we fixate.

Third, he invokes commonality by hearkening back to an ancient origin story. The image of Jesus drawing in the dirt with his hands recalls an image of God as Creator fashioning human beings from the dust of the ground with his own hands (Genesis 2:7). Literally and metaphorically, Jesus rivets attention on common ground. Later in that same creation story, the two figures God created have their own wayward moment, shaping an understanding that it is embedded in our human nature to go astray sometimes. Thus, the common ground in which Jesus anchors his response has two elements: 1) We're all made of the same stuff. This adulterous woman is no different from anyone else. 2) We're all sinners. No one is perfect, so what gives anyone the right to judge her?

## The Response

After everyone has had enough time to take a deep breath and slow their heart rates a bit, Jesus famously says, "Let the one among you who is without sin be the first to throw a stone at her" (John 8:7). The line is a showstopper. After he says it, he bends down to write in the dirt again, giving everyone a moment to process. Attention, for a second time, is focused on common ground. Sin. Whether we want to admit it or not, we are all works in progress, flawed pilgrims journeying back toward wholeness. That's our common ground. The only legitimate response anyone has is to drop their rocks and walk away.

Importantly, Jesus' response forces the Scribes and Pharisees to reconcile themselves with their own sinfulness and hypocrisies. This is where reconciliation begins. If we're not whole within ourselves, we can never be whole in relationship with anyone else or with God. We'll dig deeper into that later.

As a final note in the story, Jesus himself refuses to cast judgment upon her. This man—the only man in history believed to be without sin—refuses to cast a stone. Why? A subtext question here: Why do we continue to this day to feel we have a right to judge others when Jesus himself does not? The thing Jesus understands and demonstrates that we struggle to wrap our minds around is this: condemnation leaves brokenness; reconciliation brings wholeness. Jesus chooses wholeness over brokenness every time.

## Blowing Up the Paradigm

At the beginning of the story, the Scribes and Pharisees connive to present Jesus with only two options: adhere to the law or ignore the law. That's it. As mentioned earlier, this construct parallels our contemporary socio-political idea of conservative/liberal, right/left, red/blue, traditional/progressive.

Jesus won't take the bait. He rejects the simplicity of this paradigm straight away. One of the story's important takeaways is that perhaps we should, too.

Problem one: This dynamic is what logicians call a forced choice fallacy. It reduces all truth and reality to two overly simplified ideas, and then it suggests only one of them can be correct. But what if both are correct? Or partially correct?

What if neither is correct? What if the best solution exists on a plane completely apart from these choices?

Problem two: This dualistic approach starts from a posture of opposition and hardwires division. It demands absolute, irreconcilable separation, leaving scant room for common ground. Arguably, the paradigm is opposed to the very idea and existence of common ground and views compromise as weakness.

Problem three: It reduces imagination to a razor-thin line stretched between two opposing anchor points. It is akin to thinking the entire earth includes the North Pole, the South Pole, and the theoretical axis connecting them. Everything else—seas, mountains, fjords, daffodils, birds, everything—is excluded from consideration as though it does not exist at all. This oppositional binary notion is so pervasive that people assume common ground is some mythical midpoint between right and left, and that identifying as a "centrist" is somehow virtuous. Such nonsense! It allows no room for big-picture thinking or deep discernment. If Jesus accepted this construct, his response would have been to throw smaller stones, or fewer stones, or maybe just pelt her with olive pits.

Problem four: The conservative/liberal paradigm makes God small. Truth does not exist along an imaginary one-dimensional continuum stretching from right to left or from orthodox to progressive—a notion which politics, economics, and somehow even religion have drunkenly ordained. It's as though there is only an east and a west, with no north or south, no up or down, no breadth or depth. This mindset fosters divided, oppositional thinking rather than whole thinking. It is a sinister ruse that serves no purpose other than labeling people and limiting God. Expanding from that artificial liberal/conservative line into a 360-degree circle opens new perspectives and possibilities, but even that remains two-dimensional. Even at its smallest level, truth encompasses at a minimum all 41,253 square degrees of a three-dimensional sphere. And, of course, it's so much more than that; it's infinite in all directions and dimensions, all at the same time. Yet, we fixate on two points, one we assume to be exclusively "true" and the other exclusively "false." Talk about focusing on a tree and missing the forest! Such utter madness!

To buy into the dualistic right/left construct and to self-identify with any given point along this imaginary continuum is to subscribe to a false doctrine. It is a dark and devilish ruse that exists for no other reason than to divide people against each other.

## Reconciliation as the Promised Land

If the neighbors have stayed at your house too late and you just want to go to bed, I suggest you casually say, "Hey, I have some thoughts I'd like to share about reconciliation." I'll give you ten-to-one odds that they'll check their watches, slap their knees, and say something akin to "Oh my gosh, it's getting late. Time flies, right? Anyway, we have an early start tomorrow, so that'll need to wait for another time." Seriously, nothing slams the brakes on a conversation quite like reconciliation.

It will help perhaps if we separate *reconciliation* as an end state from *reconciling* as a process. Mostly, it's the process we eschew. We don't want to trek through the desert to get to the promised land. More on that in Part Two. For our purposes right now, let's focus on reconciliation as an end state.

Really what we're talking about is living in wholeness, united with Creator and creation. We're talking about life without conflict and stress, a life in which people encourage, comfort, and support one another. It's a way of being—reconciled as one people of God, one body of Christ—that everyone who is healthy wants.

Indeed, rare is the person who looks upon the divided, mudslinging, stone-throwing nature of our Western society and claims to prefer it or even to like it. By now, we've all experienced friendships, families, and marriages that have been destroyed by this dualistic way of seeing the world. We've seen and experienced the pain. Yet, we keep choosing to live this way. We keep animosity ripe with anger-fueled ideologies, always blaming "the other side" for the darkness, fear, and insecurity in our lives, without ever waking to the reality that we are all actively participating in creating a culture of darkness, fear, and insecurity.

No matter how righteous we believe ourselves to be, when we channel anger and hatred toward anyone, even those with whom we vehemently disagree, we contribute to brokenness and division. We allow ourselves to become conduits through which more toxic anger and hatred flows into the world and stirs into people and relationships. "Love your enemies and pray for those who persecute you," Jesus instructed (Matthew 5:44). He knew what he was talking about. Only love extinguishes hate.

The only way out of this quagmire is to refuse to participate in this quagmire. We need reconciliation more than ever.

We need it desperately, and we need it now. We need every follower of Jesus Christ to watch with riveted attention as our Messiah draws in the dirt; we need to return to the common ground of our shared origin; and we need to choose wholeness over division.

part two

# Reconciliation with Everything

3

# The Path to Wholeness

A gifted and charismatic preacher stepped into the pulpit on a sweltering Sunday morning in early August. Outside, the humid air was thick enough to muffle the endless chirps of cicadas. In the pews, women fanned themselves with church bulletins, hymn books, or anything else they could find to create a slight breeze. Men, being rather stoic, sat still, occasionally pressing handkerchiefs against their foreheads.

The preacher, a man of average height with an above-average waistline, gripped the sides of the ambo, leaned in and said in a soft baritone voice, "Everybody wants to go to heaven." He let those words hover for a moment, giving them time to land and register. Repeating them, he punctuated between the words: "Everybody. Wants. To go. To heaven."

Somewhere on the left side of the congregation, a woman encouraged him with an "Amen." Two others offered responses: "Uh-huh" and "Oh yes, Lord."

He was starting to wind up. "I said everybody, EVERYBODY wants to go to HEAVEN!"

The froth was beginning to pique. Voices called out from the community, "Amen!" "Preach it, brother!" "Alleluia!" "Say it again!"

He leaned closer to the microphone and raised his voice so it would reverberate into the parking lot: "EVERYBODY WANTS TO GO TO HEAVEN, BUT..." He let that "but" levitate in the August humidity like dense fog. The community fell silent, holding its breath. After working the room with his eyes, he brought his voice down to the gravitas of a sincere whisper. "Everybody wants to go to heaven, but ain't no one... ain't no one want to die."

## Heaven as Wholeness—Part A

Can we have a grown-up conversation about heaven? Most of us were introduced to the concept as small children, and we imagined it as a physical place beyond the rainbow bridge where there are no brussels sprouts and we're on eternal summer vacation. It was presented to us as a reward for being good little boys and girls.

Now that we're adults, let's peel back the pearly gates, sky mansions, and glitter wings for a moment and pour the wine into a clear glass so we can hold it up to the light. This is what saints, mystics, and others who live deeply spiritual lives do. They journey beyond the platitudes to have direct, personal encounters and experiences that inform and shape their understanding and belief.

An idea like heaven does not stick around for thousands of years and have profound spiritual significance unless it speaks to something universally deep within the human experience. Consider that this universally deep something for which we all yearn, this eternal bliss we call heaven, is wholeness—complete unity with Creator and all realms of creation.

This idea of a harmonious, joy-filled, fear-free eternity where there is only love draws us like tree branches to sunlight. We bend toward it, nourish ourselves on it, and soak it in even while we remain rooted in the earth. For eons, theologians, philosophers, spiritualists, and others have pondered this mystery. Occasionally, if we are truly awake, we are overwhelmed by flashing glimpses of it.

### Heaven as Wholeness—Part B

Disclaimer: I'm not a heaven expert. I've never even been there. I thought I was once when I made an amazing croquet shot across the yard, knocking my brother out of position as my ball ricocheted off his and rolled through a wicket. Dang, that was satisfying. I even said to my brother at the time, "That felt heavenly." He disagreed.

Throughout history and across human cultures, there have been all sorts of attempts to describe or imagine this idea. If you want, you can collect merchandise ranging from dish towels that quote Thoreau ("Heaven is under our feet as well as over our heads") to beer coasters that quote Mark Twain ("Go to heaven for the climate, hell for the company"). Perhaps the most cogent and comprehensive understanding is the one offered in the *Catechism of the Catholic Church* (take a deep breath, everyone): heaven is *the ultimate end and fulfillment of human longing, a state of supreme happiness and communion with God, the Trinity, the Virgin Mary, angels, and all the blessed*. Now, before your knees buckle under the tonnage of church speak, let's unpack that a bit. It's quite insightful.

Let's start by noting two things this description does *not* include. First, there is no mention of heaven being an earned reward. And second, there is no mention of temporal dimensions such as place or time. Putting those together, there is nothing in this understanding of heaven to pigeonhole it as a place we are rewarded with only after death. Instead, it is entirely compatible with the words in Mark's Gospel where Jesus says, "The time is fulfilled, and the kingdom of God has come near" (Mark 1:15).

I'll be the first to wince at heavy-handed religiosity, but ponder for a moment what the Catholic Catechism is saying. Heaven is the sublime experience of being one with God and all creation now and forever. Who among us doesn't want that? This communion, this oneness, this ultimate union with Creator and creation—this is wholeness.

## A Nod to Skeptics

If you're thinking, "Oh, come on, dude! No one really knows anything about heaven or if heaven even exists. You're merely justifying a religious narrative," well, good for you! Seriously. Those with the deepest spirituality often have the deepest doubts. Questions and skepticism can be gifts that urge us ever deeper into mystery beyond the shallows of reason and comfort. By all means, please, keep challenging. Keep seeking.

To clarify, however, I am not merely justifying a religious narrative. Hang with me: we are headed toward common ground. I am reconciling the religious narrative (heaven) with the spiritual experience (wholeness). These are not separate or distinct things. Whether you're someone who is moored in the Church and seeks a deeper relationship with God, or you're someone who starts with a walk in the woods and seeks a deeper experience and encounter with mystery, we're all pilgrims on a path toward wholeness with Creator and all creation. Hopefully, we can all be open to one another so we can walk together and grow with each other.

## Ain't No One Want to Die

If you're astute—and clearly you are, since you've chosen to read this rather than rewatch season three of *Farmer Wants a Wife*—you're likely rubbing your forehead with one hand and tugging at metaphorical reins with the other while thinking, "Whoa, Meyer. Roll this buckboard to a slow stop. If heaven is available to us in the here and now, why would we have to die before we can get there?"

That's a brilliant question. Thank you for asking it. We have a lot of mixed-up language and references about death. It's easy to confuse ourselves. Consider the story of Jesus raising Lazareth from the dead. He tells Martha, "I am the resurrection and the life. Those who believe in me, even though they die, will live, and everyone who lives and believes in me will never die" (John 11:25–26). Well, that's clear as mud, but it's exactly the sort of language around life and death we need to untangle. Note: sometimes "untangle" can be a synonym for "reconcile." Many of our divisions are often just misunderstandings.

My mother often said that life is about letting go. We just keep letting go of things until we are finally ready to let go of life itself. In many ways, the mystery we call death is just another term for letting go. Wholeness—a state of complete happiness and communion with Creator and all creation—is not something we attain through acquisition; it is a state we enter through subtraction. Only by letting go of things such as ego, prejudices, insecurity, fear, and self-importance are we able to transition into communion with wholeness. Stated more familiarly, we must die to rise.

The problem, of course, is that we don't want to let go. We invest our entire lives building up ego rather than letting go of ego. We justify prejudices, hedge against insecurity, protect against fear, and advance self-importance. Rather than defining and shaping ourselves by a love of God and love of neighbor, we cling to all the things we would be best off to release. This happens because we let our egos trick us into thinking we can achieve happiness by changing the world around us. If I can change laws, change policies, change minds, change others' behavior—basically, if I can get the world to conform to my liking, then I will be happy. In reality, we can only enter the state of supreme happiness and communion with Creator and creation by changing the world within us. Everyone wants to be whole, but no one wants to let go of ego and self-importance. Everyone wants to change the world, but no one wants to change themselves. Everyone wants to go to heaven, but ain't no one want to die.

4

# The Wholeness of Creation

Toward the end of Margaret Atwood's novel *Surfacing*, the story's protagonist digs a hole in the earth, sheds all her clothes, and rolls in the dirt, covering herself with the dust of her own creation. It is a stark, avant-garde conclusion to her journey quest toward wholeness. When I first read this novel as a college senior, I didn't really get it. I thought the ending was a little weird. Although, to be fair, a lot of things were beyond my comprehension in my early twenties, including wearing socks. I read it as the character becoming less human and more animalistic.

As a student of literature, I understood that she was ritualizing a reunion, a reconciliation of sorts, with her one true nature. But I didn't understand the fullness of the metaphor. She gains the wholeness of herself by becoming one with her Creator and creation. She isn't becoming less human; she is becoming more of everything. Arguably, she is reuniting with her inner Eve. It is worth noting that it is in this state that she finally is able to open herself to feelings of love.

## Whole at Creation

Speaking of Eve, even if you aren't at all religious and read it simply as an important piece of cultural literature, the second creation story in the Book of Genesis is brilliant. Here, in the first book of the Bible, God—who is later identified in the Bible's last book as the Alpha and the Omega, the first and the last, the beginning and the end (Revelation 22:13)—fashions humanity from the dust of the ground. In other words, The All of Everything (Alpha and Omega) handcrafts humanity from stardust, the energy-turned-matter substance of the universe.

You and I are made from the exact same stuff as pear trees and microbes and salamanders and koalas and distant planets and moons. If you think this is all a bit too hippie-dippie or New-Age-esque, I gently remind you that the story predates written history and is a timeless anchor of the Judeo-Christian lexicon. Besides, much of what the lululemon crowd embraces as "New Age" is actually rooted in ancient Jewish and Christian mysticism. Shh... don't tell them; they're not ready to hear it yet, so let them believe they've discovered something for themselves. Either way, the ancient creation story is worth a deep look. It is chock-full of ancestral wisdom that has shaped human history. The All of Everything creates everything from all of everything. So, yes, of course, we are made in God's own image and likeness! I don't think we sit and meditate on that enough. If we did, we'd sure treat each other better.

Hang on, it gets even better.

After creating people from dirt, God blows the breath of life directly into this human form. Poof! Right in the nose. Pause and ponder what this means. Our very lives are animated with God's own breath! Holy cats! That should blow the hair right off your head! Try not to get bogged down in the metaphysics or quantum theory of all this. Instead, release your mind to the mystery and the pursuit of spiritual truth. The Alpha and Omega, the infinite source of all life and love, created you out of stardust and breathes life in you and through you. I mean, wow! How's that for unitive wholeness with Creator and creation? It really can't get more poignant.

By the story's end, we have two people, Adam and Eve, both created from carbon and nitrogen and given life by God's own self—the Alpha and Omega, the All of Everything. And what are they doing? They're living in the harmonic wholeness of full unity with Creator and creation. It is, shall we say, heavenly.

## The Rise of Individualism

There is a saying in Eastern philosophy that if you want to know something, you must go to its opposite. If you want to truly appreciate light, you must experience darkness. If you want to value joy, you must experience despair. If you want to know love, you must experience loneliness and isolation. Thus, it follows that if we want to fully understand the value of unity and wholeness, we must experience the consequences of individualism.

So, Adam and Eve sneak a bite of the ol' apple. Why? They are tempted by the self-aggrandizement of individualism. Why should they share in God's knowledge and wisdom when they can have their own? Why should they settle for being one with the One when they can become number one within themselves? Why be content to be stardust in the universe when you can be the star of your own universe, however small that may be?

In Christian parlance, we call this original sin, but it's a concept that seems so archaic it rarely even gets mentioned. If you want to be the person everyone talks about for days after the party, go ahead and bring up original sin. You'll never get invited back, but most certainly you'll be remembered. Yet, this is the proverbial core of the apple. It's the human tendency to want to go it alone, to believe the myth of the self-made achiever, to want to be master rather than servant, and to put ego-interests ahead of the common good. Jesus had a lot to say about this, and it wasn't favorable. Nonetheless, there is a part of each of us that likes original sin. We like putting ourselves first before all others. In fact, we sort of like making little gods of ourselves. We can scapegoat Adam and Eve all we want, but most of us sink our own teeth into that apple every day.

## The Consequences of Individualism

The conventional interpretation of the Adam and Eve story is that a wrathful, punishing God kicks the duo out of Eden for eating the forbidden fruit. It's harsh discipline for violating a seemingly arbitrary and arguably petty rule. What's more, all of humanity is thereby also exiled to a life of suffering and toil as further perpetual punishment. Holy overkill!

As a quick aside, perhaps the most tragic part of the story is that generations of people today miss the point. We take this beautiful piece of allegorical storytelling, a story that was passed down through a hundred generations via oral tradition before it was ever written down, and we either regard it as historical fact or dismiss it as historical fiction. In either case, we miss the point. It wasn't passed along through generations to document fact; it was passed to ponder truth. And it wasn't written down to record history; it was written down to preserve timeless insight.

Among other things, that timeless insight includes this: toxic individualism alienates us from wholeness with Creator and creation. Exile from Eden is not a punishment, it is the inevitable consequence of self-centeredness, of elevating the self as an individual above all others, or as my firefighter friend, Paul, says, "Suffering is what happens when you live to put *me* before *we*." When a cell within the body goes off on its own and does its own thing, it becomes a tumor. It will destroy the entire body to feed its own growth.

As a note of clarification, God never asks humanity as personified by Adam and Eve (also by you and me) to neglect the self. We are encouraged to pursue unity and harmony, not self-denial. "Love others *as* yourself," Jesus said. He didn't say, "Love others instead of yourself." One of the by-products of dualism as discussed in chapter 2 is a default tendency to see everything in terms of opposition rather than unity, so we insert *or* into every relationship: either I put others first *or* I put myself first. That is a forced choice fallacy. We readily forget that healthy spirituality is whole. The *me* is included within the *we*. The grape becomes one with the wine without losing its own value.

## Reconciling with Creation

Since the dawn of time, when we humans first became aware of the concept of "self" distinct from Creator, we have hungered for a return to wholeness; we have thirsted for reconciliation between Creator and creation. This is what we live and die for. More than anything, we yearn to be one with the One. This is our true nature. We have been handcrafted from stardust in the image and likeness of the One who created us, and we have been brought to life by the sacred breath of Holy Spirit. We all know—when we stand and welcome the sunrise, when we hold an infant in our arms for the first time, when we walk in the woods after a rainstorm or let the surf lap our bare feet—on a spiritual level, we all know that everlasting joy is only found when we are reconciled and unified with our origin.

This is inherent in the perennial truth common across time and cultures. Native American religions are built upon this understanding of oneness with creation. Eastern religions integrate it. And it is a foundational, but oft neglected, cornerstone of Christian spirituality, as thinkers no less than St. Francis will attest. As the inspiring Christian mystic Julian of Norwich noted, "The Goodness that is Nature is God. He is the ground, He is the substance, He is the same thing that is Naturehood. And He is very Father and very Mother of Nature."

Indeed, living in oneness with Creator and creation is our nature. Yet, we keep choosing to live in brokenness. We want unity, but we choose division. We want harmony, but we choose duality. We want peace, but we choose antagonism. We want to pursue healing, but we perpetuate hurting. Again and again, we keep choosing to live contrary to our own true created nature.

The trailhead on the path to wholeness starts with the realization that we have a choice. We can choose to journey toward unity, harmony, healing, and full reconciliation with Creator and creation. Or not. We can choose to live as one in the wine or shrivel like individual raisins.

5

# The Wholeness of Incarnation

In 1988, as the world was awash with advertising icons like the California Raisins and the Energizer Bunny, a Scottish duo named The Proclaimers released a song called "Gonna Be" (aka "500 Miles"). It took five more years before the song was released in North America, but when it finally was, it rocketed up the Billboard Top 100. The rhythm and melody were infectious, but the lyrics had a magnetic quality that drew your head and heart together and wouldn't let them separate.

"Gonna Be" offers testimony as to how devoted the singer is to the person he loves, how far he would go to be with her. Not only would he walk five hundred miles, but then he would walk five hundred more—why? Just to be the man who walked a thousand miles to collapse in front of her door. That's love. The very idea: to walk to the ends of the earth and completely exhaust himself just to be with someone he loves. Sound familiar?

No one is going to claim this is a Christmas song. Except me. How far will God go to erase the distance between heaven and earth, between Creator and creation? How far will God go just to be with us and among us? To the ends of the earth.

## So Much More Than Jesus' Birthday

In the last chapter, I asked if we could have a grown-up conversation about heaven. You kindly obliged and everyone survived. Now I'm asking if we can have a grown-up conversation about Christmas. I realize this request is a tad more delicate. People tend to have a more sacred hold on Christmas than on heaven. By *Christmas* I mean *incarnation—God becoming flesh, the Alpha and Omega becoming one like us, with us, among us, and within us*. It's odd that we need to clarify that Christmas is about something spiritually profound.

Not to diminish the merits of angel-shaped sugar cookies and the Hallmark Channel, but, man, have we taken the spiritual significance of incarnation to the shallow end of the pool! In the book *Living with Real Presence: Eucharist As an Approach to Life*, I introduced the term "theological reductionism." It was the best way I could think of to describe our tendency to take profound theological and spiritual concepts and reduce them to a level seven-year-olds can understand and then leave them at that level. Celebrating Christmas as "Jesus' birthday" is another example of theological reductionism.

Let's settle something quickly before outrage crashes social media: I love Christmas, and I'm all in on celebrating the birth of Jesus. Of course! I am neither Scrooge nor Grinch. What I am saying is that incarnation is so much more than that. While we hang lights and tinsel on the *what, where,* and *how* of Jesus' birth, we barely give a nod to *why* he came into existence. The *why* is everything, and the trope "to open the gates of heaven" is a bone without meat (unless we understand that "heaven" is wholeness in unity with Creator and creation starting right now). Christmas is an event, but incarnation is a reality. More specifically, incarnation is a realignment, a reconciliation that restores our unitive oneness with God. And while Christmas is a day or maybe even a season, incarnation is forever.

## Let's Put This in Context

Since the dawn of time and the rise of individualism, our Creator has continuously called humanity back into wholeness, back into unitive oneness. Many of the iconic Old Testament heroes and prophets dedicated and sometimes sacrificed their lives to reunite humanity with God. Arguably, the entire biblical history prior to Jesus is about the human tendency to go our own way and then get called back.

Well, God got tired of waiting for us. I'm paraphrasing here. Nowhere in Scripture does it say God got tired of waiting for us. I'm not being fair to the infinitely patient Deity. But that pretty much captures the upshot. Humanity has not been able to make its way back to unity and wholeness with the One whose breath fills our lungs, so the One unifies with us. If we stubbornly and staunchly insist on retaining our independence like foot-stomping thirteen-year-olds, refusing to get in the car with the Alpha and Omega, then the ever-loving, ever-patient Alpha and Omega says, "OK. But I love you too much to leave you alone. So I'm coming to be with you."

It's like the line in "Hark! the Herald Angels Sing," the one that states, "God and sinners reconciled." That's the whole deal.

## Set Jesus Free

Every year in my community, and I'm sure in yours, too, there is a committed group of people faithfully beating the drum to "keep Christ in Christmas." They post messages on social media and put all sorts of stickers on their cars. All's good. They're pushing back against what is perceived to be the commercialization or perhaps secularization (that's a problematic word—more on that later) of Christmas.

But that's not the problem. The so-called War on Christmas is a gaslight that feeds a needless sense of controversy, dividing people at a time intended to unite people. There is no systematic, much less organized, effort to take Christ out of Christmas. In fact, Christmas is the one time of year when people, including a lot of Christians, actually pay attention to Christ and live differently because of it. Seriously. People visit nursing homes, give generously to Toys for Tots and Coats for Kids, bake cookies for their neighbors, stock food pantries, and go to church. Yes, Christmas is the one day each year when our churches are full. People get in the Christmas spirit, the Christlike spirit, and care about each other. More or less.

No, the problem isn't that anyone is locking Christ out of Christmas; the problem is that we lock Christ inside Christmas and keep him there. We love our neighbors for a day or two, maybe even a week or two, but then we go right back to our old self-interested, ego-centric behaviors. By January second, we're flipping the bird to people in traffic, cursing our coworkers, and ignoring the homeless. We turn toward unity and wholeness for a day, then scurry right back to division and fracture.

## Live It Like You Believe It

It's good to have a day that brings out our best and shows us who we are capable of being. That's Christmas. But what's the point if it doesn't change us? What's the point if we love one another for a day, but then live "me first" for the rest of the year? Celebrating the birth of Christ as an event allows us to contain Christmas within a season and not let it really affect the rest of our lives. Do you see how messed up this is?

Incarnation—a fifty-cent word with a million-dollar meaning—changes the way we see ourselves and one another. And that changes everything. At least it ought to. Once we fully accept that the living, breathing God is with us, among us, between us, and within us, we are able to live with jaw-dropping awe every moment of every day. Incarnation brings all of creation into harmony and erases the distance between humanity and God, between heaven and earth, between Creator and creation. It heals all fractures and makes us whole. If we let it.

As a kid all charged up with sugar and a lack of sleep, I got a little surly and started a fight with my sister one Christmas. I don't remember exactly what I said, but I may have suggested that her intelligence was akin to the east end of a reindeer flying west. My mother overheard this. Oops. "I can't believe you would say something like that to your own sister, especially on Christmas!" she chastised. I found her response curious because she knew me, and it was exactly the sort of thing I'd say to my sister, so why did she find it hard to believe? In retrospect, though, her words expressed two problems with our Christmas logic that would be reconciled if we fully embraced incarnation.

First, she said, "I can't believe you would say something like that to your own sister." Think about that. Would it have been less wrong if I had said it to someone who was not a sibling? Of course not. Incarnation inspires awareness that we are all brothers and sisters living in sacred unity with this Triune God. All humanity has been reconciled with the One who is the Alpha and Omega; there is no more separation. This is true of every single person, including the least among us, as Jesus points out.

Second, my mom said, "Especially on Christmas." These words perpetuate the notion that we should act differently on Christmas than on other days. This sort of defeats the point, doesn't it? Incarnation calls me to love all people all the time, because, again, all people are included in the unitive wholeness reconciled by incarnation.

6

# The Wholeness of Eucharist

When I was a kid, my mom made the bread for our family. From scratch. We were spoiled. I'm not talking about the pre-made cheater loaves purchased in the freezer case and popped in the oven. Nor am I talking about throwing some pre-packaged ingredients into a bread machine and then pouring a glass of wine while you wait for the magic. She made it with her own hands and heart, just like her mother and her mother's mother before her. The only shortcut my mom took was in not milling her own wheat. She bought Gold Medal flour in ten-pound bags, and it was my job to empty the bag into an old-school flour bin outfitted with a crank-operated sifter. And, no, I am not *that old*; my mother was *that authentic*.

Once a week, she would hoist the massive slab of a breadboard onto the kitchen table and get to work. And I mean work. The sleeves were rolled up. The rings came off her fingers. And she dug in, mixing and kneading. And kneading. And kneading. She worked that dough with the accomplished finesse of an artist and the powerful tenacity of a blacksmith. Then she would cover it with a blanket and set it by a window where the warm sun would inspire the yeast. When the dough had risen beyond the containment of the tub, she would plunge her fists deep into the mass to release the air. As a fifth grader, I started calling this *farting the bread*, hoping it would catch on. It didn't.

The neighbor kids loved bread-baking day at our house. They would hang out and watch the dough rise with fascination. And when the loaves came out of the oven, we'd drizzle honey from my grandfather's farm on warm slices. It was candy on a cloud. I don't know if I have ever tasted anything better.

Without realizing it at the time, my spiritual development was being hewn by my proximity to the origin of my nourishment. I saw the bees and the hives, and I watched my grandfather harvest honey from combs. I watched my mother work the bread dough with her own hands and saw it rise in the sun. The bread of my life brought people together. It linked family, neighbors, and generations of ancestors. It even connected me with the wheat in the field and the bees in the garden. Years later, when I was introduced to the Buddhist teaching *when you drink water, remember the one who dug the well*, it seemed obvious to me. We emerge in wholeness through our awareness of connection and communion with Creator and creation.

## One Bread, One Body

The Passover that Jesus celebrated with his friends connected them with each other and with their ancestors. The very context of this meal was communal, and they would have understood it as such as they reclined and leaned against each other. So, when Jesus took bread and wine right from the table—fruits of the earth and work of human hands—they would have comprehended the inherent oneness of it all. These were Jewish people who understood that the God they knew as Elaha, YHWH, I AM was the All-ness of Everything, the source of life that flowed through their own blood and put air in their lungs. When Jesus held up a loaf and a cup and said, "This is my body; this is my blood," they would not have seen it as metaphoric or symbolic. They would have fully recognized it as literal, material, emotional, spiritual, existential, and theological. In unity with Jesus, they all became part of the Oneness of God, as do we.

Likewise, when Jesus says, "Do this in memory of me," they would have understood that he was not merely asking them to repeat the motions of the ritual. He was instructing them to live out the meaning of the ritual: come together and return to wholeness by reconnecting (reconciling) with me, with each other, with God, with creation, with the All of Everything: become one Body of Christ. With that in mind, recall Jesus' prayer for universal wholeness:

> "that they may all be one. As you, Father, are in me
> and I am in you, may they also be in us, so that the

> world may believe that you have sent me. The glory that you have given me I have given them, so that they may be one, as we are one, I in them and you in me, that they may become completely one, so that the world may know that you have sent me and have loved them even as you loved me." *(John 17:21–23)*

Upon first reading, this may seem like a nonlinear, circular, and almost somersaulting prayer that leaves your brain in knots. The logic is hard to follow. But root yourself in an understanding of Eucharist as Jesus actively breaking himself open and pouring himself out so that he can become one with us and we can become one with him—all of us together as one fully reconciled Body of Christ, erasing the distance between all duality, between Creator and creation, between God and humanity, between heaven and earth, and restoring wholeness.

## Do This in Memory of Me

He could have walked away, you know. When he was in the garden before the soldiers showed up, Jesus could have shaken his head, thrown his hands in the air, and said, "The heck with this. I'm out." That's what most of us would have done. And who would have blamed him? He had given his entire life to his mission and nothing had really changed. Not a single institutional injustice had been corrected; not a single policy or practice had even been examined, much less changed.

People heard him and gravitated toward his message, but apparently not enough to live differently because of it. The poor were still being exploited. The money changers were back to changing money. The temple authorities were still in cahoots with the Romans. And even his closest followers still ego-bickered about who was the greatest. Peter would deny even knowing him. Judas was in the process of selling him out to line his own pockets. And the people for whom he had just broken himself open and poured himself out were in wine-infused food comas and falling asleep.

He could have walked away. After all, there was nothing in it for him. It's what most of us would have done.

But Jesus did not live by the rules of individualism, the ego-economics by which we score everything based on what's in it for me. Jesus did not evaluate his effort from the same self-investment mindset our Western way of life has normalized. He wasn't the sort to leave a vocation, a relationship, or a religion because "You know, I'm just not getting out of it what I'm putting into it." He lived as a servant of God's kingdom, not as a beneficiary; as a contributor, not as a consumer. And he contributed everything. Every heartbeat. Every breath. He gave his own all-of-everything to reconcile and reunify all of humanity with the Oneness of God. And then he said, "Do this in memory of me."

7

# The Wholeness of Resurrection

I'm not sure how many times I've died. A lot, probably. It's hard to add them up, especially since they're all fractions. A big part of me died when my father passed away. Years later, I'm still discovering pieces of myself that left this life with him. My youthful sense of immortality, for example, escaped this earth when he did. At the same time, though, I keep finding pieces of him that are being brought to new life in me. My father had a way of keeping things in perspective that I couldn't grasp in my youth and I envied in middle age. But now, in the years since he died, I am guided by his level-headed voice resonating from within myself. It would be easy to dismiss this as merely the wisdom of aging, but we all know better because we all know plenty of folks who have not become more level-headed as they aged.

Each time one of my sons left home to go off to college, part of me died. It left a hollow emptiness once filled with the life of a father and son sharing Lego and soccer and the first-time ascent of a mountain summit. Even now I tear up with the ever-ripe grief of lost forts in the woods and the candy bars we'd sneak into our Home Depot cart, telling each other it's a guy thing and Mom didn't need to find out, even though we both knew she would ask, and we wouldn't lie. Still, though, even the small deaths along life's journey yield to the creative force of new life. I have adult relationships with my sons now, relationships filled with humor, sawdust, and deep conversations about mystery.

If I've learned anything in my many lives and deaths as both a son and a father, it is this: there is no point on earth or in heaven where my life stops and another life starts. Through life and death and life again, the love we share entwines us like the strands of a single cord. We are all made stronger and whole by braiding ourselves together in collective singularity, in holy oneness with Holy Oneness. And no matter how many parts and pieces of us die along the way, we are always and inevitably reconciled and made whole with a life-force love that never dies.

## Quick Recap, Part 1

Caution: I'm going to wax a little church-nerdy here, but take solace in knowing I don't like it any more than you do. First, though, I'm going to pass along the advice I received from an old Benedictine monk many years ago: scrape off the foam so you can taste the beer. In other words, clear away the highbrow language of religion as well as the dismissive filters of objection so you can ponder the deeper mystery. Let's begin with a review of what got us here.

First, the spirituality of creation is rooted in our unitive Oneness with the All of Everything, the God we call the Alpha and the Omega. It advances the beautiful and brilliant idea that human persons are created in the image and likeness of the Creator, using the energy-converted-to-matter of stardust or, more colloquially, the dirt of the earth. We are all made of the same stuff as everything and each other, and we are animated to life by the very breath of our Creator who, again, is not merely a being, but Being itself, the great I AM. And this is all very sacred. Indeed, if this isn't sacred, arguably nothing is sacred. Separating creation into the sacred and the secular is a disservice to the Creator who created it all, and it sets up yet another false and divisive duality. Earlier, I mentioned that I strongly dislike the word "secular," and I promised an explanation would come later. Well, here it is. Once you embrace the infinite reality that all is of God, you understand and appreciate that all is sacred. There is no *secular*, and insisting otherwise inevitably narrows God from One to *some*. The fact that we think individually and partially rather than wholly does not alter this.

Second, humanity is apt to separate itself from the harmony and unity of creation by yielding to the temptations of ego and individualism. Sometimes we disengage from our wholeness with Oneness and become the smallness of one. When cells in our bodies lose their sense of collaborative purpose and do their own thing, we call it cancer. When people do it, we call it sin, a term we often avoid because it feels archaic and gives us hives, but the concept remains timeless and applicable.

Third, the history of spirituality and religion which has threaded across time and cultures is essentially humanity's universal desire to restore the sacred wholeness of our creation. We use phrases such as "return to God" and "go home to heaven," but what we mean is to become one with Oneness, to be whole with the Alpha and Omega.

## Quick Recap, Part 2

If you've been rolling your eyes dismissively at all this, you haven't yet blown all the foam off the beer. Give yourself a gift by taking a deep breath or two or ten, courageously stepping beyond the dimensional realm of rationality, and opening yourself to the deeper mystery of spirituality. Remember, compassion is not rational. Gratitude is not rational. Hope is not rational. Falling in love, sacrificing your own freedom for your children, crying at graduations, none of it is rational. All the very best things that make life amazing live beyond the realm of rationality. OK, back to our reset.

Fourth, as Christians, we believe incarnation manifests God's loving desire to reunify with us, to close the gap between Creator and creation, between heaven and earth. Perhaps that's a little heady? Sorry. Let's go back and release the word "incarnation" from the shackles of church speak. Bottom line: lured by the siren songs of ego and individualism, we humans tend to go our own way and separate ourselves from the whole—like a baseball player who values personal glory more than team victory and refuses to lay down bunts or hit sacrifice flies. Therefore, in the interest and pursuit of wholeness and communion, God humbly becomes one with humanity. That's incarnation.

Fifth, before his death, Jesus gives us Eucharist, a gift so unitive that we call it Holy Communion. In doing so, he breaks himself open, pours himself out, gives himself to us so he can be one in us, we can be one with him and with each other, and together we can all be one body of Christ.

We could take all of this into much richer and far deeper discussion, but for our purposes here let's summarize it as this: our entire Judeo-Christian spiritual tradition points to our wholeness and oneness with God, who self-identifies in the Book of Exodus as "I am that I am" (existence itself) and self-identifies in the Book of Revelation as "the Alpha and Omega" (the all of everything).

## So, What's the Point of Reconciliation?

All should be good, no? We had unity in the beginning. Then we invented division and separation. But then incarnation reconciled creation back with the Creator, so all is restored, right? The gaps between God and humanity and between heaven and earth have been erased. So, what's the problem?

One huge gap remains—the gap between life and death, between our earthly temporal realm and the infinite realm beyond dimension. Resurrection closes that gap, reconciling the dimensional with the non-dimensional, the temporal with the infinite, life before death with life beyond death.

The idea advanced in our faith tradition that Jesus had to die so he could rise to new life is an insightful expression of Christian spirituality. It can feel like a lot of trite church speak, but blow off the foam for a sec. There is a deep and profound spiritual truth being revealed to us: by letting go, we release ourselves to growth. By letting go of our prejudices, we release our hearts to grow into wholeness with others. By letting go of our notions, we release our minds to grow into deeper connection with truth. By letting go of our pain and trauma, we release our spirits to grow beyond the iron bars of brokenness. By letting go of ego and individualism, we release our souls to grow toward reconciliation with all creation. Ultimately, by letting go of this finite life itself, we release ourselves to expand into the infinite wholeness of Oneness.

Without this gift of resurrection, ultimate reconciliation or reunification would be impossible. God may have closed the gap through incarnation, becoming one with humanity, but one final element of brokenness remains until we come full circle and the created willingly return to oneness with the Creator. Thus, it can be said that those who believe in Jesus as the resurrection and the life shall never die (John 11:25–26).

part three

# The Way of Healing

# 8

# Reconciling with Self

Michelle and I sat together on the brown couch in a counselor's office. We held hands and authentically loved each other, but still there was a wall between us, a wall we had mutually built from opposite sides. I leaned back and tried to look comfortable and confident. This—the very fact that I felt a need to posture myself in a way that was contrary to how I honestly felt—was at least part of the reason we were there. Life is hard enough, and marriage can make it even harder. But life can also be enriching, enlivening, and rewarding, and marriage can make it even more so. The trick is in dealing with your own baggage and not dumping it on your partner. We were both dumping but didn't realize it yet.

"Marriage would be so much easier if we were gods and not humans," a friend once told me. I wanted Michelle to see me as godly. She most certainly did not. We each had carried our own humanity into the relationship without understanding the gnarled complexity of it. This included personal, familial, and ancestral histories of pain, joy, suffering, compassion, addiction, healing, insecurity, empathy, shame, forgiveness—basically, all the stuff that makes humans so human. Research now shows that trauma tags genetic markers and can be passed from one generation to another, manifesting in future generations as anxiety, depression, and other such yuck. Think about that. It gives new understanding to the biblical claim that the sins of the father are laden upon the children (Exodus 20:5). It also makes my grandfather (who was the son of a raging and violent alcoholic) very wise for instructing us to deal with our own trauma because our children will carry enough of their own.

## Naive Innocence and Myopic Arrogance

During our early years together, Michelle and I could readily overcome conflicts because, like many young people, we saw ourselves, each other, and our relationship through rose-colored glasses. In our hearts and minds, there was nothing our love couldn't make perfect. At that life stage, our love was like young wine with a label that promised a full note that the vintage couldn't yet deliver. Mostly, we were in love with images and notions of who we wanted to be—and who we wanted the other person to be. That's not at all fair, if you think about it, yet we tend to do it to each other all the time. We create an image of who or how we want other people to be, and we hold them accountable to that image, choosing to like or dislike, to approve or disapprove accordingly. I can't imagine this is appreciated by the Creator in whose image all those other people have been created.

We weren't fully honest with ourselves or with each other about who we were because we didn't fully know ourselves. We were each trying to be the person our formative influences—teachers, peers, parents, clergy, and employers—thought we should be, which isn't always aligned with who we were each created to be.

Then reality hit. The pie-eyed unicorns of youth were quickly slain by cranky children, middle-of-the-night vomit, backed-up sump pumps, and unexpected car repairs. Our unreconciled inner conflicts leaked through in how we responded to outer conflicts. We began assigning our own insecurities and self-conflicts onto each other as though life would be more harmonious and less stressful if we could get the other person to change.

Therein lies the root of nearly all conflicts and stress in our lives: the mistaken belief that our lives would be less stressful and less broken if other people would change. Here's a spiritual wake-up: you will never become whole by changing other people. Also, you cannot change other people.

## From My Perspective

I rolled my truck into the garage shortly after six. It had been a long and stressful day because, as it turns out, the people with whom I worked were also human and hadn't dealt with their own brokenness, either. We had a lot in common. More than anything, I wanted to step through the door into a home that was a sanctuary, where children played joyfully and cooperated with each other, and where my bride would welcome me with delight.

It sounds embarrassingly immature and self-centered, which is fair because it was. In my weak defense, Michelle had wanted a quasi-traditional situation where she primarily stayed home with the kids, working outside the home only part-time or not at all. We both understood and agreed that this would mean I'd have to work extra hard and extra long to build a career capable of financially supporting the family. So, whether I deserved it or not, I felt a little entitled to come home to a sanctuary filled with peace and joy. After all, I reasoned, I was busting my tail to support her dream.

Instead of going in, I sat in my parked truck and took a few deep breaths. This wasn't a unique day; it felt like every day.

I needed to collect myself and prepare. A reality awaited inside the house that would be very different from my idea of how things ought to be. There would be no refuge, no tranquility in which to center and unwind. The kids would be hungry, crabby, and tired from a day at school. Someone would be emotional about something that happened at lunchtime, someone would be stressed about his homework load, and someone would have locked horns with his mother.

Michelle would be in the kitchen, stirring resentment into a pot of rice. She'd be frustrated with the kids and, instead of being glad I was home, she'd be upset that I hadn't gotten home earlier to support and help her. We didn't have a marriage; we had a functional partnership in which I was valued only for a paycheck and respite services.

### From Michelle's Perspective

I gave and gave and gave. Every time I turned around, someone wanted something from me. My time was never my own. The responsibilities of caring for the kids and running the household were endless. Steve got to go off to his office every day to do his own thing. When he traveled for business, sometimes he'd be gone for several days, eating in restaurants and drinking wine, leaving me at home to take care of everything. And I mean everything. The least he could have done is come home from work on time. But he would show up late and then... and then sit in his truck in the garage for ten minutes while I was inside trying to wrangle kids and get dinner on the table. Get in here and help!

My stomach felt tight almost all the time. I never got enough sleep. The entire household and family relied on me. I was responsible for everything, yet everything revolved around his schedule. When he came home, he expected me to be this joyful, loving wife, but I was exhausted. He wanted downtime? Tell me about it! When did I ever get downtime?

When he finally walked through the door at the end of the day, it was chaos. The kids would come running and were all excited to see him, but honestly sometimes I was not. Sometimes I think it was easier when he traveled because at least I knew what I was dealing with. He walked in on his own timeline and thought I was somehow supposed to invent a magic hour out of thin air where he could unwind while we had some sort of relaxing conversation before dinner. It's like he was living in an alternative reality and entirely oblivious to this one. We didn't have a marriage; we had a functional partnership in which I was merely the caregiver, cook, laundry lady, cleaning lady, and ride service.

## Brokenness Starts Inside

The first counselor we saw gave us tools and advice for managing our marriage and being more in tune with each other. It helped for a bit. But there is a difference between managing a reality and solving a problem. The friction between us, even the mutual resentment, was not the real issue. It was merely a symptom. The second counselor we saw helped us see that the real problem was that neither of us were whole. We both had unreconciled brokenness that needed to be addressed. We needed to stop projecting our own crud onto the relationship and deal with it ourselves. Note: the correct professional term for residual brokenness is not "crud." But it should be.

## The Source of Our Own Conflicts

For Michelle and me to grow forward into a union that would be whole and harmonious, we each had to first work on reconciling our own inner conflicts. Perhaps this is the insight Jesus is sharing when he tells us to tend the wooden beam in our own eye before pointing out the splinter in the other person's eye. Deal with your own crud.

I've grown to believe that many, if not most, of the conflicts in our lives and in our world are the inevitable projections of our own inner disconnects and disharmonies. How can we possibly be whole in relationship with anyone or anything else when we are broken and conflicted within ourselves? Instead of doing the spiritual work of admitting brokenness and pursuing wholeness, we keep acting out and projecting onto others, even those we love the most.

## Ego-Self vs. Authentic Self

We've touched on this a bit, but it warrants a strong underscore here. From the time we become self-aware, we are surrounded by voices that affirm us when we conform to expectations and condemn us when we do not. The kid who scores the goal is lauded. Report cards with A's are hung on the refrigerator. We are told to "make your parents proud," and the resulting accolades and attention when we do are addictive. Many of us come of age with our entire sense of self-worth hinging on the approvals of others.

It is common for people to reach middle age with a robustly encouraged, developed, and defended ego-self, but no real sense of the authentic self. We just keep looking for external validations of our egos in whatever form helps us feel good about ourselves. For some, it's position and prestige, always vying for the next rung on a ladder. For others, it's material in the form of fashion, cars, or homes. Some find it in the achievement of academic degrees or athletic accomplishments or the number of social media followers. There are some among us who even find it in a sense of moral superiority and religiosity, showing the world that we're somehow better than sinners who are less religiously inclined.

Eventually and inevitably, our ego-self comes into conflict with our authentic self. The person we self-create in our minds is at odds with the person the Alpha and Omega created from stardust and breathed life into. We can only ignore the person we were created to be for so long before the shallowness of the ego-self is exposed. Sitting in that room with the counselor, Michelle and I were each awakened to the reality that we needed to let go of the voices in our heads telling us who we ought to be, and we needed to listen deeply to the spirit voice calling us to be whole in and of ourselves. That takes a lot of spiritual and emotional work. But it's worth it.

9

# Reconciling with Others

Jorge assembled his team around the conference table, being intentional to sit midway along one of the sides. He never sat at the head of the table, reasoning that he would rather lead from a position of authenticity than from a posture of authority. He looked up and made brief eye contact with each person before beginning. “What would you all say if we hired Cami back?” he asked.

There was a collective startled gasp followed by silence. “Wait. What?” someone finally said. “Why on earth would you do that?”

“Well,” Jorge began, “we have a great opportunity with Archer Enterprises, but there is one piece missing. Cami. The client really likes her, loved working with her in the past, and she has a particular skillset our team is lacking. It could be a win-win-win. Archer gets a great fit, we get a great piece of business, and Cami gets to do what she’s most gifted at.”

"Frankly, I'm surprised you'd even consider it," Will spoke up. You could always count on Will to say what everyone else was thinking. He had been with the firm for nearly twenty years and was secure enough in his position to speak his mind. "I mean, come on. Cami didn't exactly leave here on the best of terms."

"That's putting it mildly," Aubry added. "She signed off with a giant middle finger pointed directly at you, Jorge. If I remember correctly, she spent months afterward telling everyone who would listen that you're the biggest A-hole in the industry."

"Yeah, that's true," Jorge acknowledged. "But she didn't mean it. She was going through a dark time and needed someone to blame. I was the obvious target."

"She sure sounded like she meant it," Will offered. "She repeated it many times to many people. Dragged your name through the mud and piled manure on top of it. The more I think about it, the more shocked I am that you're even asking about hiring her back."

Jorge possessed the type of settled gravity that anchored a room without having to speak. He leveraged it here, allowing silence to hold the moment. "She and I have some things we'll need to reconcile before this could happen," he finally said. "I'm still here and expectations haven't changed, so she'll need to be OK with that. But you all know Cami, right? You worked with her for several years. She's a good egg. You all liked her, right?" Around the table people nodded. "The way she left—that wasn't her," he continued. "We don't know what was going on in her life at that moment, but we all know her exit was out of character. That wasn't the real Cami. If we don't judge her for who she was in her worst moment, but instead consider who she always was before then, would you be able and willing to work with her?"

Around the room, postures opened and relaxed. "Look, Jorge," Will said, sensing he was speaking for everyone, "the only real beef I have with Cami is the way she left. She screwed up and tried to blame you for it. But if you can forgive her, then the rest of us sure in heck can. Give her a call if you want and see if she'll come back."

"Can I be on that call?" Aubry kidded. "Because that girl is going to be shocked to hear from you."

## What Happened Next

When Jorge called Cami, she almost didn't answer. Seeing his name pop up on her phone reignited unhealed pain and momentarily stopped her breath. Her stomach stirred with weird knots. She had enjoyed working with him and his team for eight years, and she had established real friendships, but she grew to resent the way Jorge insisted on growth and continuous improvement. To her, it felt as though he didn't think her work was good enough anymore. Jorge had assured her that wasn't the case. He had tried to explain that the industry was changing, and she was at risk of falling behind, but she took it as a personal affront. So, when another opportunity presented itself, she jumped at it.

Unfortunately, her departure wasn't her best moment. The flattery of another offer boosted her ego, and from that perch she unleashed her frustration in the form of an insult storm. Nearly a full year later, she regretted it and tried to put the whole thing in the past. But now Jorge's name flashed on her screen. The firm she joined had filed for bankruptcy, and she was out of work. She couldn't afford to cast off any lifelines, so she answered.

After a few awkward pleasantries, Jorge explained the purpose of his call and asked if she might be interested in returning. Cami was dumbfounded to the point of being tongue-tied. When she finally found her words, she said, "Well, yes. Thank you. I'd be very interested, but are you sure? I would not have expected this."

Jorge was forthright, "You and I go back a ways, Cami. I've known you for a long time, and I've seen you at your best and at your worst. When you left... well, that wasn't your best. You said a few things that didn't reflect well on either one of us. I need to know you're past that."

"Yup, that's fair," she said. "You're right. That's not who I am, and I've wished I could take it back."

"Cami, you called me the biggest A-hole in the business, and you need to know I'm still here and I haven't changed. We're going to still expect you to stretch yourself."

Cami's response was quick. "No, I wouldn't expect you to change. But I have. I've learned some things. You were right; the industry was passing me by. I know now that you weren't being critical, you were being helpful. I was stubborn and complacent."

## Master-Level Reconciliation

The relationship between Cami, Jorge, and the rest of the team was able to return to wholeness because of three advanced dimensions of reconciliation: 1) respect for the human journey, 2) focusing on the positive rather than the negative, and 3) honesty and vulnerability. These go beyond the basic apology and forgiveness formulation we were taught as children, a prescription which is still helpful in a lot of ways. But life gets complicated, and brokenness can be complex, so reconciliation can require mature soul searching and spiritual self-awareness.

***1. Respect for the Human Journey*** Once when backpacking in western Colorado, we ended a long and arduous climb by crossing over a ridge at about 11,500 feet. On the other side would be a beautiful alpine lake teeming with cold-water trout, where we would camp and, hopefully, feast. As we trekked across the ridge, we were greeted by a massive herd of beef cattle that had somehow grazed its way up from the opposite valley over the course of the summer.

I don't know how familiar you are with the bovine diet and digestive tract, but in the interest of delicacy, let's just say it's productive. They eat a lot of roughage. And they process a lot of roughage. That's just how the Creator created them. The entire lake basin was populated with mooing cattle and rich, moist, impressively pungent post-digestive residual. It was a mess.

Circumstances being what they were, we had little choice but to find the best available spot and set up camp anyway. At first, I found the whole situation upsetting, and I was filled with resentment. I had hiked up a mountain to find tranquility, only to be dealing with massive piles of... let's call it organic byproduct. As I tried to salvage some sort of life lesson from this, it occurred to me that if we're going to share life with other beings, we're just going to have to put up with their byproducts sometimes. For me, finding harmony became as simple as forgiving cattle for being cattle. Likewise, in life, finding harmony is often as simple as forgiving humans for being human. From time to time, we all discharge emotional, arrogant, mindless, insensitive byproducts that other people have to navigate and occasionally step in.

Life is messy. It just is. We are often willing to give ourselves a break, understanding that we go through good times and bad, navigating the peaks and valleys of our human journey, but we struggle to extend the same understanding to others. Among the things I personally learned from my time working with Jorge was to embrace the reality that everyone is on a journey toward wholeness, which also means none of us has arrived yet. None of us is finished. Authentically loving another person means supporting and companioning them on that journey, accepting that their brokenness is going to show up some days.

Obviously, we need to give ourselves safe distance from people who are abusive, destructive, or dangerous in some way. In the mountains, we steered clear of the bulls. We needn't tolerate another's brokenness to the point of our own peril. To paraphrase Jesus, we might need to kick that dirt from our sandals and move on in such cases. Perhaps the other person's journey needs to wander through the desert for a bit and confront its own demons, and we can best serve them and ourselves by keeping a little distance.

In the majority of our encounters and relationships, though, it helps if we draw a distinction between an episode and a trend. When Peter denies knowing Jesus, it was a moment of weakness, an episode. It wasn't his pattern of behavior. The wholeness of his relationship with Christ was able to be reconciled because Jesus recognized that Peter's human journey would inevitably swerve off the road and crash into the ditch sometimes. For many of us, these are the human errors that enable us to learn and grow.

In reconciling our relationships with others, especially people who may have said or done something that was inconsiderate or even hurtful, we acknowledge their humanity and respect their journey. In other words, we forgive them for being human just as we expect others to forgive us.

***2. Focusing on the Positive Rather Than the Negative*** Bruce Taylor, my Advanced Creative Writing professor, passed out a thin packet of papers. He started every class by distributing a few select samples of student submissions from the previous assignment, and if yours was among them, you'd be expected to read it aloud and then listen to the collective observations, affirmations, and criticisms as the class discussed the work. If the packet was thick, there would be several pieces; he wouldn't be intending to spend a great deal of time on any of them, perhaps emphasizing only a point or two. If the packet was thin, containing only two or three samples, it meant he anticipated going in-depth on at least one of them.

I received the packet and immediately noticed it was unusually thin. I then saw that the first piece of work was mine. I swelled with quiet pride. Apparently, this writer and professor who I respected so very highly had deemed my short story worthy of sharing and discussing in depth. When I finished reading it to the class, Professor Taylor eschewed his normal process of opening it to general input, instead addressing me directly.

"Let me ask you about this Patrick Kreely character," he began. "How do you feel about him?"

"He has some personal problems that he turns into problems for other people," I replied, still a bit confused by the poignancy of the question.

"Mm-hmm," he replied. "That doesn't answer the question I asked. How do you feel about him?"

"I guess, I mean, I based the character on an old boss I had who..."

"Do you like him?" he interrupted. "Do you like this Patrick Kreely character?"

I didn't have to think about it even for a moment. "No. I don't like him at all. I think he's a small and arrogant man."

"That's obvious. My question to you, Mr. Meyer, is how dare you? How dare you create a character to serve your own purposes as a writer and then have the audacity to dislike him? You made him. You gave him his thoughts, his words, his actions, and his responses. You did all of that, but then you held him responsible for it. How dare you?" I sat dumbfounded and embarrassed, but this man I held in such high esteem was just getting warmed up. "Even God loves all the people he created, even the ones who seem small and arrogant at times. God still loves them. But you don't? Do you think you're better than God?"

I sank to the floor, my ego a puddle that was being lapped by worms. Ugh. Bruce Taylor went on to give an absolutely brilliant lecture that changed me and my life. Decades later, I think of it often and am still so deeply grateful for the lesson. He spoke of character development specifically, but of humanity more generally. "There are no perfect people," he told the class, "Which means no one is perfectly good or perfectly bad. Make sure your protagonists have flaws and be sure to give your antagonists redeemable qualities. Otherwise, they won't be real." Then he added, "People are neither good nor bad. They might do good and bad things, but we are all just imperfect people trying to navigate our way through life. Good writers recognize this and don't judge anyone."

When Jesus looked upon the ragamuffin Peter, the Samaritan woman at the well, the tax collector Zacchaeus, the blind, the lame, and the lepers, he didn't judge them for their imperfections and flaws. Instead, he focused on their redeemable qualities. He saw the positive rather than the negative. While none of us are Jesus, we are all capable of making that same choice.

***3. Honesty and Vulnerability*** Seth, a Lutheran pastor and friend of mine, tells of the time he became emotionally vulnerable after blowing a gasket with his teenage son. He lost his cool and absolutely exploded in a way he now describes as his most failing moment as a parent, but the exposure of his fragile humanity became transformative. He tears up and his voice cracks when he tells the story, making his vulnerability ripe again and again.

The way Seth tells it, his son Luke was a kid doing what kids do. In reality, he was eighteen years old, which is hardly a child, but Seth claims that only means he was a kid who had stopped admitting he was a kid. Few over the age of forty would disagree. In Seth's words, Luke wasn't doing anything he hadn't done many times before over the previous three years; he was battling his father for an upper hand.

It was a familiar dance. The son played offense, pushing buttons, arguing every one of his father's responses, and crossing the line into personal affronts. Seth regarded his role as defense, to remain stoically unwavering, unfazed, calm, and collected as he countered Luke's sticks and stones with patience and reason. But Luke had become adept at manipulating logic for his own purposes, and he was all too eager to draw blood with his sharpened teeth.

Coming off an awful day, Seth had neither the energy nor the disposition for his son's rebellion. More than anything, he wanted to shut the world out. No sooner had he crashed onto the couch when Luke launched an aggressive opening.

"Where were you all day that was so important that you didn't have time for your family?" he asked with an accusatory sneer. In his mind, he was speaking out in advocacy for his mother and younger siblings. It was spring break, and Luke was home from college. Seth had taken a few days off to spend with the family but had worked all day, and Luke was holding him accountable.

"I would have much rather been here with you," Seth replied with a resigned sigh. He hoped that would be the end of it.

"If that were true, you would have been," Luke retorted. "Why don't you just admit that your lame church stuff is more important than your kids?" He said it with the raw edge of a disguised joke, as though he thought cutting with a dulled knife wouldn't break the flesh.

Seth was in no mood for feigned jocularity. Not this night. "Wow. You know that's not true. There is nothing more important to me than this family. And what I was doing today was not lame." Luke was luring him in and had already gotten him on defense, but Seth was too emotionally spent to see the quicksand. This is the point at which a voice told him to get up and walk away, but he didn't listen.

"Of course it's true. The evidence clearly shows you had a different priority today, and that's lame."

"It's not that simple."

"Yes, it is that simple." Luke didn't know about the phone call his father had received late that morning, nor did he know about the police officer on the other end.

"Can we please not do this right now? Just let me be. Please?" Seth could feel all the air pushing to the top of his lungs. His muscles were tightening. What do you do when the fight or flight response is triggered but you lack the energy to do either?

"What's the matter? You're gone most of the day and when you finally show up, we're all supposed to leave you alone?" Luke was coming strong and didn't yet have the maturity to see his father's humanity.

"Dude, just knock it off, OK? I can't... I just can't."

"You can't what? You can't be bothered to be a decent father and spend time with your kids?"

That's when Seth says he lost it. He sprang from the couch and got in his son's face. The entire day, the history of tension in his relationship with his own father, memories of two different classmates he had known in high school who had taken their own lives, it all flashed to the fore and exploded on his own son. "Damn you!" he screamed. "I asked you to leave me alone, to let it go!"

Consumed by overwhelming emotions, he grabbed his son by the shirt and started to lift him off the chair. Suddenly aware that he was no longer in control of his emotions and fearful of how this might escalate, Seth released his son and ran from the room. And he wept.

As soon as he caught his breath, he was consumed by sadness and shame. How could he have done that? How could he have treated his son that way? Seth loved Luke at depths beyond measure, and he would willingly bleed out and die for him. What damage had he done to this sacred relationship? Was there a way back, a way to unburn the bridge? Immediately, he went to find Luke, but his son reached him first.

"What's going on?" Luke asked. "Are you OK?"

"No," Seth confessed with tears running from his eyes. "I'm not OK."

"This is not like you at all. What's going on?"

Seth reached for him with both arms—this amazing human person who had been created in the image and likeness of the Alpha and Omega, this brilliant young man with the heart his father envied and the mind he revered, who had been brought into his life eighteen years earlier so that he might steward and nurture his growth. Now roles were suddenly reversed and the son held his father.

"It was a suicide," Seth said. "I spent all afternoon with a family who..." He choked on the words, searching for the wind needed to free them from his throat. "They found their son hanging in the garage this morning. He was, he was nineteen. That's where I was today."

"Shit," Luke whispered. "I'm sorry."

In that moment, their relationship transitioned beyond the built-in power roles of father/son. For the first time, they experienced mutuality. Luke got to see his father's human brokenness and share his own strength. To be healthy, relationships require such mutuality. Thus, Christ becomes one of us, broken and vulnerable. Reconciliation is very difficult, if not impossible, when one person maintains power or superiority over the other.

They embraced again. Seth apologized for losing his cool and for being gone much of the day, and Luke apologized for not respecting his father's appeals. The most important part, though, is that Seth let go of his ego need to be seen by his son as strong and stoic, and he let his son see his tears and hold his vulnerability.

Christians revere the image of Christ crucified, broken open, and bleeding out. He lets us see his vulnerability, his fragile humanity. This is where all reconciliation with fractured relationships begins—this willingness to be honest about our own fragility and to be vulnerable with those with whom we are in conflict. And then we must immediately respect and revere the sacred vulnerability of the other. For any of this to be possible, we need to live beyond the tight-fisted grip of our own egos.

10

# Reconciling with Humanity

We love Lego bricks in my family. That's a bit of an understatement. It's an obsession; arguably, an intergenerational addiction. Michelle and I have three sons, all adults now, and all are even more enthralled with Lego than when they were kids. When the oldest was five, I read about research comparing Lego kids and video game kids, the upshot being that kids who preferred playing with Lego bricks tended to develop better imaginations and problem-solving skills than those who spent their childhood playing video games. A lot has changed since then, and video games have become far more complex and sophisticated, so there's a good chance those findings no longer apply, but as a young father at the time, that's all I needed. I went overboard.

Lego for birthdays. Lego for Christmas. Lego all summer long. A large portion of our basement was home to an extraordinary Lego city, complete with a comprehensive citizenry of Lego characters who had been assigned personalities and occupations. The city had its own economy, monetary units, and political system. Storylines were created. Movies were shot and edited.

Each of the kids brought his own personality and imagination to Lego City, and the result was a rich tapestry of simulated humanity. There was a mayor named Mr. Rich who spent all his time glad-handing people on the streets, a hotspot pizza parlor that may or may not have bought and sold black market oregano, and even an organized crime syndicate that slashed tires so people would be forced to get repairs at a certain service center. Through the years, there were innumerable invasions by space aliens, requiring the city to come together to rebuild itself. Anything was possible.

## A Unifying Force

Our three sons were spread across eight years, so when the eldest was thirteen, the youngest was only five. In addition to being at different stages of growth and development, they all had very different interests, opinions, and personalities. Oh, and they were all competitive. Most games would spiral into giant fights, as the two who were losing would conspire to manipulate or even rewrite rules to bring down whoever happened to be winning. Things got ugly.

But Lego City was different. It was a collaborative and cooperative creation that brought the boys together rather than tearing them apart. In fact, at Christmastime they would combine their gift requests around what they agreed Lego City needed. Michelle and I were limited in our budgeting, so this meant they would voluntarily curtail individual gifts to get what they could share together.

Three boys. Three personalities. One city. City Council meetings were held, negotiations could last days or even weeks, and deals were made. Lego City expanded, growing from a single plywood sheet to a multi-platformed extravaganza with trains, skyscrapers, parks, and a lake. When the city outgrew its borders, suburbs sprung up in other parts of the basement.

Without realizing it and without parental direction, the boys discovered the power and joy of unity. They each contributed whatever imagination and creativity they could to create something far more awe-inspiring than what any of them would have achieved individually. Through it all, however, they somehow understood that the thing they were creating was secondary, merely an expression of the far more important thing they were experiencing and sharing: brotherhood.

## Serving a Common Good

Lego City worked because it was not the most important thing. The WHAT (Lego City) was never more important than the WHY (relationship). The infrastructure, politics, and economy of the object existed to serve the relationship between the people, and ultimately to serve the greater good of all, bringing peace and joy to our home. Just pause and think about that for a moment. It's the foundational basis of community, this idea that by working in wholeness and harmony we can advance relationships and the common good. Bees living in a hive get it. Ants in a colony get it. Even trees living in a forest get it. Why do humans struggle so much with this idea of unitive purpose and oneness?

This core belief that the common good outweighs personal self-interest is an axiom of nearly all forms of Eastern and Western spirituality. Within the Christian tradition, we believe it is why Jesus submitted to crucifixion. His example may be a little more extreme than most of us would hope to be asked to emulate, but it clearly demonstrates an important tenet of wholeness: each of us is here to serve a good greater than self.

## Choosing Brokenness

Imagine for a moment if the boys building Lego City prioritized individualism over brotherhood. What if the object became more important than the purpose, or if the purpose shifted to focus on individual priorities rather than brotherhood? There would be arguments and turf wars. Each would hoard bricks. There might even be sabotage. Before long, they wouldn't trust each other at all. There would be "winners" and "losers" and, with it, there would be fights and fracture.

When we choose to prioritize our individual self-interests over the greater good of the community, we contribute to systems that inevitably create conflict and brokenness. We choose the smallness of one over the greatness of the One, and in doing so we pave a wide highway for the seven deadly sins: pride, greed, wrath, envy, lust, gluttony, and sloth. This is true in communities as small as family units or as large as nations and states. It even happened within the community of Jesus' apostles when they bickered over who was the greatest. Jesus addresses this by instructing that the one who is the least is the greatest.

I want to be clear about two things before moving on. First, I am not suggesting that the needs and interests of individuals ought to be ignored or even relegated. Each person has gifts that can serve and benefit the greater good, and the whole community is best served by nurturing and encouraging those interests and talents. Second, I am not here to advance an agenda for systemic change through social policy or law. Arguably, there is need and opportunity for such change—I am not discouraging it, but my purpose is to encourage a change of heart in the tradition of John the Baptist who advised us to repent (change). This is first and foremost a spiritual endeavor, not a political or economic one. That being said, I invite you to ponder whether the current state of political and economic polarity could be reconciled by a spiritual awakening.

## The Roots of Social Brokenness

We seem to be living in an extremely stressful time. Anxiety is almost an epidemic, even among schoolchildren. It appears that nearly everyone lives on a knife's edge, one hat-drop away from personal or social collapse. Why? None of us wants to live this way. It's not the life experience we hope for, nor is it the world we want for our kids. Yet, here we are, not even realizing we have a choice or that we are contributing to this dynamic.

Stress and anxiety trick our mind into thinking something is amiss, that danger is afoot. Such perceived threats trigger a primal instinct for self-preservation, causing us to become even more self-concerned and self-focused. In other words, stress drives us deeper into the grips of individualism, causing us to mistrust and fear one another more and more. To make it worse, a continuous toxic stream of political programming and social media is stoking the fires, as investors have figured out how to monetize and profit from anxiety and animosity. If there is one thing that makes our time in history different from previous eras, perhaps it is that people have figured out how to turn fear and hate into a product they can sell for money. I'm certain corporate executives would argue with me, but this is largely how talk radio, 24/7 cable news, and social media drive profits.

Instead of building communities of love and contribution, we're riding individualism toward fear and consumerism. The default litmus for all decisions ranging from spiritual practice to public elections is "What do I have to gain?" and not "What do I have to give?" We consistently choose personal security over loving vulnerability, leading to a society with more people carrying more guns, building more walls, and living behind more locked doors. We are choosing to live in fear of one another rather than in love for one another. Why? Going back to the Lego City discussion, we have changed our purpose from brotherhood to individualism. In Christian parlance, we have chosen to take up the sword rather than the cross. And harkening back to chapter 4 in this book, we keep choosing the apple over Eden in an attempt to turn ourselves into little gods.

## Reconciling with Society

As I mentioned earlier, my mission in writing this book is to nudge hearts. This is where the journey toward wholeness must begin. Only through changing hearts, each of us starting with our own, will we have any real hope of changing the world. This does not devalue social justice efforts, nor does it diminish the role of political activism. After all, we are called to work for justice, feed the hungry, give drink to the thirsty, shelter the homeless, and do all the other Corporal Works of Mercy. But we can do all those things—indeed, a lot of extraordinary people are doing those things every day—and still have brokenness and division in our relationships with society.

If we're going to heal what divides us and move closer to unity and wholeness, I suggest we each commit to a five-part Social Wholeness Code:

***1. Lead with Love.*** Make the Creator's love (the unitive wholeness that forms us from stardust and puts breath in our lungs) the most important arbiter of all your social decisions. Whether interacting with an argumentative coworker, passing an unhoused person on the street, or checking a box on a ballot, ask yourself two simple questions: What is the most loving thing to say? What is the most loving thing to do?

Be careful: you're going to want to manipulate this to justify a preconceived position. Sometimes when people bring brownies or other baked goods into work, I will say, "Gee, Bonnie would be offended if I did not have any. But she will feel complimented and appreciated if I really enjoy it, so I should probably have a very large piece. Yes, that's the most loving thing to do." You see what I did there? It's easy to manipulate love logic to justify self-interest. One can easily say, "I love my family, so the most loving thing to do is to hoard my money and build generational wealth so my grandchildren never have to stress or toil."

Remember, we're talking about God's love, which is always generous and unitive. It helps if we self-identify as a conduit through which the Alpha and Omega seeks to bring more and more love into creation. From that perspective, ask yourself, "What is the most loving thing to say?" and "What is the most loving thing to do?" This is how Christ lives through us and seeks to bring healing to a fractured world.

***2. Tend the Beam in Your Own Eye.*** No one likes to do this. I get it. It's uncomfortable. Our egos would much rather criticize others than work on our own selves. It's much more self-satisfying to pontificate about everything that's wrong with "society" than to address whatever is holding us back from fully loving God and neighbor.

That's the real spiritual question, isn't it? The true examination of conscience: What's holding me back from loving the Creator and all creation with my whole heart, soul, mind, and strength? Hint: the answer is not "other people." It's not liberals or conservatives or immigrants or atheists or skateboarders or dysfunctional parent figures or anyone else. It's something within the self. That's the giant beam in your own eye that needs tending.

In my own experience, there was a time when insecurity and judgmentalism held me back. I looked at other people and, instead of seeing the sacred expression of God they were each created to reveal to the world, I saw myself in comparison to them. I was like the self-righteous Pharisee in the parable who looked judgingly upon the tax collector in the temple area as I said, "God, I thank you that I am not like so many other people who are greedy and dishonest." Instead of seeing their sacred humanity, I selfishly saw how it reflected my own, judging them for being better or worse (whatever that means) than I was. Social comparison is a dark business. I could always find a way to tint my lenses so I could feel better about myself. How much better it is, as Jesus points out, to be like the tax collector in that same parable who simply says, "God, be merciful to me, a sinner!" (Luke 18:13). That guy was tending the giant beam in his own eye, something I needed to deal with before I could ever hope to reconcile myself with all of society.

***3. Be a Disciple by Practice, Not by Proxy.*** Our social media culture and obsession with the political landscape have given us the illusion that we can be Christian disciples by getting other people to think what we believe they should think or to do what we believe they should do. We expend extraordinary energy working the churn through prayer, posts, and politics, calling for other people to be inspired to do good things. But when Jesus gets done washing the feet of the disciples, he says, "I have set you an example, that you also should do as I have done to you." (John 13:15). He does not say, "Go and fight for politicians who will pass mandatory foot-washing laws."

As I mentioned earlier, this does not preclude the value of advocating for social justice. Not by any means. But we are called to be disciples of action, to be Christians through practice, not through proxy. Slapping bumper stickers on our cars and planting signs in our lawns might trick us into feeling like we're doing something, but in reality we're not. As a college freshman during the height of the Cold War, I became aware of the dangerous build-up of the global nuclear arsenal. My response was to hang a "Peace is the Answer" sticker in the rear window of my car, which was the only form of social media we had way back in the 1900s. And that's fine. I was trying to help build awareness. But that's all I did, and it wasn't enough. I still harbored animosity toward people who saw things differently. I routinely looked for debates, intending to crush others with my self-perceived superior knowledge and arguments. Without realizing it at the time, I was contributing to a culture of conflict and animosity. I certainly wasn't practicing what I was preaching.

If I've learned anything in my work with unhoused people on the streets, it's the full meaning of the idea that the gospel is most effectively shared through action, not through words. Truly, if we have any hope of social reconciliation, we would be wise to worry less about bringing people to Jesus and focus more on bringing Jesus to people.

***4. Be an Agent of Wholeness.*** Stepping aside from his profile as the Son of God for a moment, one of the most compelling things about Jesus as a human being was how open he was to everyone. He dined in the home of a prominent Pharisee as well as that of Zaccheaus the tax collector. He sat with the Samaritan woman at the well and with the Scribes in the temple area. He simply refused to accept or conform to the social divisions of his time. He'd have none of it. Instead, he saw each person as a sacred expression of the Creator, and he did not see them in the shadowy light cast by human conventions such as economic or social status.

We each have it within us to make the same choice. We can advance social reconciliation by being agents of wholeness rather than division, people of communion rather than conflict. We can reject the onslaught of voices demanding that we conform to the artificial construct of a conservative/liberal paradigm. We can advance wholeness by loving God and neighbor, by valuing and defending the least among us, and by forgiving others as we are forgiven ourselves. And we can expand our sacred imagination to create avenues of reconciliation with all humanity rather than pursuing resolutions that advance self-interest.

***5. Draw in the Dirt.*** In chapter 2, we discussed the value of hitting the pause button, refocusing our thinking, and rooting ourselves in common ground. The way Jesus responded to the Pharisees who presented him with the woman caught in adultery is a master class in reconciling social conflict. He didn't merely resolve the issue; he brought reconciliation to the moment and to the community by rejecting the dualistic forced choice presented to him, and subsequently by re-establishing wholeness.

Taking time and making space to draw in the dirt is akin to a spiritual hazmat suit. Without it, emotional toxins with names such as fear, hatred, animosity, and selfishness enter our bloodstream like the viruses they are.

As the fault lines of social division surround us with fractures, we would be wise to figure out how to personally draw in the dirt. For Jesus it meant being silent, bending down, and literally touching the earth, which as we previously discussed also had the powerful metaphorical value of reconnecting with the substance and wholeness of our creation. But what does it mean for you? How do you draw in the dirt? However you personally do it, it likely involves the same basic elements: silence, getting in touch with the substance of your own creation, and focusing on common ground.

## Fair Warning

You could do all these things to reconcile social divisions and still end up on a cross. It happened to the best of us. That's the risk we take.

11

# Reconciling with Creation

Michelle and I were walking through the woods holding hands, listening to songbirds, and smelling the air like we were in a Hallmark movie when she spotted a pair of monarch butterflies flitting among a stand of violets. Sometimes earth gives us a momentary shot at Eden if we open our eyes. It was a brilliant display of orange and purple among a sea of springtime green. Truly, God's creation inspires awe when we slow down to notice. There are between 17,500 and 20,000 different species of butterflies in the world. Imagine that! And there are as many as 400,000 species of wildflowers! Remarkable! Clearly, the Creator's imagination is boundless.

Without claiming to know the mind of God, I think it's safe to say our maker intends to gift us with variety. There are over 35,000 identified species of fish, and we keep finding more. And insects? It is estimated there are 5.5 million species of them, but who really knows? Our brains cannot begin to comprehend the vast wonders of this amazing creation or of its Creator.

The real beauty of creation is seen when we look at the entirety of a forest, pond, desert, or any ecosystem. So many different plants and animals live together harmoniously in a symphony of collaborative give-and-take. Plants produce oxygen and nutrients needed to sustain the life of animals, which in turn produce carbon dioxide and nitrogen needed for plants, while all sorts of insects and microbes continuously turn over life cycles. From earthworms to eagles, the whole is so much greater than the sum of the parts.

St. Paul underscores this "nature of God" when he writes to the Corinthians and explains that although we are many parts, we are one body. While we each have different gifts we are called to share through different forms of service, we are united in a good so much greater than any of us individually—the unitive Oneness of God. This idea, which was emphasized by St. Augustine in the fourth century and St. Hildegard of Bingen in the eleventh century, is so foundational to Christianity that Pope Leo XIV has made it his motto: *In Illo uno unum* (In the One, we are one).

One of the most fascinating parts of the Pentecost story highlights this diversity. When the Holy Spirit descends upon the disciples, they each start speaking in different tongues (Acts 2:4). Clearly, it is within the power of the Holy Spirit to inspire all people to speak and understand a common language. All things are possible with God, but instead of uniting through homogeny (making all the same), our Creator unites through diversity.

## Infinite Wonder

From the delicate wings of dragonflies to the jaw-dropping vistas of sunsets, the marvels of creation stir and inspire something within us. Who can gaze upon a single dew drop hanging from a spider's web and not be awed? In addition to providing the fruits that nourish us, the water that sustains us, and the air that animates us, the wonder of creation serves as muse for the art, music, and poetry that lift humanity closer to the heavens.

Who among us has not felt closer to Oneness when gazing into a starlit night? We take vacations so we can escape our human-created chaos by sitting in boats on calm lakes, walking shorelines with waves lapping our feet, or climbing mountains and sleeping among the trees. When we want to "get away" and "clear our heads," we seek peace and tranquility in nature. Indeed, research shows that looking at trees reduces our stress levels and lowers our heart rate. There have even been studies showing that people staying in hospital rooms with windows that look out at trees tend to recover faster and have shorter stays.

## So, What's the Conflict?

If we are made of the same stuff as the earth and stars, totally dependent on the bounty of creation to sustain our lives, awed by the inspiring beauty of nature, and drawn closer to Oneness when immersing ourselves in creation, what's the conflict? What is there to reconcile?

Allow me to offer three fractures crying out for spiritual wholeness: 1) a power struggle, 2) a consumer mindset, and 3) short-term thinking.

***1. Power Struggle*** Wild Man Don and I had backpacked over three days to an alpine lake just below the summit of Cloud Peak in Wyoming's Big Horn Mountains. Allow me to pause and introduce you to my brother-in-law, Wild Man Don. His name is Don—I added the "Wild Man" part partially out of irony, because he is an extremely buttoned-up accountant, and partially out of respect because he is most at home in the wilderness and has earned the title. At 12,500 feet, we were feeling a little on-top-of-the-world smugness. After all, we had conquered a mountain!

Then, out of nowhere, a huge storm rolled in. To be clear, given that we were at three thousand feet above the tree line, with nowhere to seek shelter, this storm did not roll over us; it rolled at us, around us, and even under us. Powerful winds whipped. Lightning flashed. Thunder shook the ground. And driving rain pelted us like buckshot. It was as though the Alpha and Omega was saying, "Feeling smug, eh? Let me show you something."

The wonders of creation humble us. They knock us to our knees and remind us again and again how vulnerable we are and how fragile life is. As it turns out, however, the human ego does not like being vulnerable. We love standing atop the mountains we've climbed, posing with the fish we've caught, or showing off the roses we grew and saying to ourselves and others, "Look what I did. I conquered nature." Compare that to the rituals of our native brothers and sisters who, after a successful hunt, offered prayers of thanksgiving for the animal that had just given its life for their survival. On second thought, don't bother. Our ritual is ego-advancing; their ritual was humble.

Even in the aftermath of natural disasters from hurricanes to wildfires, from tsunamis to pandemics, people point fingers, looking for someone to blame. We demand to know whose fault this is, what system failed, why we weren't warned. We could choose to come together, acknowledge the shared vulnerability of our human condition, and then respond with generous compassion for the victims. We could use these occasions to become more loving, unified people. And, in fairness, sometimes we do. Sometimes. But more often, we choose to respond with politics, using the occasion to divide people and advance human power agendas.

As a result, we are locked in a power struggle with creation and the Creator, a power struggle we will inevitably lose and are, in fact, in the process of losing. Yet, we stubbornly and arrogantly keep biting into the apple.

***2. Consumer Mindset*** Let's open our minds a bit and consider the Garden of Eden narrative as the introduction of consumerism into the human experience. Stay with me here. The story features two characters, Adam and Eve, who live in wholeness and harmony with Creator and creation. Life is heavenly. There is no *us and them*, no *heaven and earth*, no duality at all. Arguably, this is humanity's most natural state, the way of life to which we yearn to return. This privileged life of wholeness and bliss, however, comes with one stipulation: the parts must submit to the whole, otherwise it doesn't work. All the life forms in the garden, including the two humans, live in mutuality and symbiosis with all the other life forms. Many parts, one body. Adam and Eve, having been created in the image and likeness of the Alpha and Omega, are the designated stewards of this ecosystem. In this role, they are servants, expected to lead by example.

In the middle of this garden sits a metaphor in the form of a tree, a symbolic presence reminding Adam and Eve that the life of the garden is not theirs to do with as they please. There is a limit and an order to things. The garden belongs to God, the one belongs to the One, creation belongs to the Creator, not to them. And while they are certainly a part of it, they are stewards, not masters.

Of course, they're tempted by the idea of becoming God-like themselves. As we mentioned earlier, this is the birth of individualism. They put ego and self-interest above all else. (As an aside, let's not portray them as victims of the serpent's cunning wiles. The serpent has no power they don't willingly give it. In fact, the serpent's only ploy is to play to their egos, and they readily eat that up even before biting the apple.) What happens next is critical. They decide that all the fruits of creation are theirs to do with as they please, that they can consume whatever they like to feed their own self-aggrandizement. And with that, we have the birth of consumerism.

To this day, this same conflict continues to play out in our relationship with creation. On one hand, we have this built-in awe and reverence for the majesty of the earth and the heavens, while on the other hand we readily exploit it as a resource to be owned, consumed, and even pillaged for profit. Instead of self-identifying as beings with a responsibility to serve and steward the whole, we elect to self-identify as masters with a right to lord it over the whole. We think creation is ours, all the while forgetting that creation belongs to the Creator.

***3. Short-Term Thinking*** Try to imagine the infinity of time and space. It's crazy. We can't begin to wrap our heads around it. Our frame of reference is confined to three dimensions and defined by earth years, so our imaginations are simply too small. But don't give up. Push your boundaries a bit. You don't have to think far to realize how small we really are and how brief our time on earth is.

In the endless expanse of the All of Everything, the I AM that is infinite Being, our individual lives barely register as a momentary flash of light. Individually, we are blips. It is only in our union with the timeless, boundless, infinite whole that we are part of true and lasting greatness. For this reason, we must die to self and be raised to eternal life. By ourselves, we are nothing. In God, we are one with everything.

Recognizing that we are temporary stewards who have inherited responsibility for the earth from our ancestors and will pass it to future generations, many Native American cultures invoke a seven generations doctrine. They contextualize all decisions with a sense of respect to the generations that have come before and obligation to the generations that come after. By doing so, they see their own lives as a point in the ever-flowing continuity of creation rather than the be-all and end-all of creation.

Our individualistic orientation dupes us into thinking and even believing that creation's story arc piques during our personal lifetimes. This short-sightedness comes packaged with time-blinders, enabling us to shrug our shoulders as we plunder earth's resources, pollute the oceans with plastics, and smother the atmosphere in greenhouse gases, all in the name of profit and convenience in the here and now.

## Returning to Common Ground

One would think that reverence for creation would be baseline common ground, certainly among those who identify as children of God. Throughout human history, people of all ilks and stripes have found solace in nature and inspiration in the stars. In the open air, the Holy Spirit sings to us, filling our lungs with the sacred breath of the God-self. By nature we are conceived and born. By nature we live and breathe. By nature we die and rise. The Franciscans even suggest that creation is God's first incarnation, the original expression of the God-self, and that Jesus Christ is the second incarnation.

Somehow, though, we have made the accumulation of wealth and the achievement of luxury a more compelling priority than reverence for creation. In making our relationship with creation an economic interest rather than a moral imperative, we have made it a point of political divide, buying into the forced-choice fallacy that we must either support economic prosperity or environmental stewardship.

Reconciling our conflicts with creation requires us to realign our priorities and reconnect with our common ground. Can we agree that it is in the interest of the greater good, including future generations, to acknowledge our oneness with and dependency on creation? Can we allow our universal human needs to breathe clean air and drink safe water to be a point of unity rather than division? Can life on earth for all creation be prioritized over wealth accumulation for a few? If not, then we must wonder if we have become the money changers whose tables Jesus overturns.

12

# Reconciling with God

If you ask a four-year-old, “Where’s God?” she’ll grin wildly, squint her eyes, and point to her own heart and then probably to yours as well. If you’re lucky, she’ll giggle and pinch your nose playfully. You’ll hold her tightly, wanting this moment of pure love, this quick flash of heaven, to last forever. She will have answered your question not with words but with experience. And you will cling to it with all your life because it is the last time she will answer the question so insightfully.

If you ask her again at the age of eight, “Where’s God?” she will look seriously and point to the sky while saying, “In heaven with Grandpa.” Existentially and metaphysically, she’s not wrong, but that’s not how she understands it. Somehow, in four short years, God moved from within the human heart to some esoteric, nebulous realm that we can’t access until death. That seems like a long way to travel in a few short years, even for God.

And if you ask again when she turns twelve, "Where's God?" she'll shrug her shoulders and run off to kick a soccer ball with friends, almost entirely unaware that God is alive in the love she shares. I once asked one of my sons at the age of twelve, "Where's God?" and he looked straight at me and said, "I don't know, Dad. Why don't you retrace your steps? I am not responsible for keeping track of where you left God."

Here's the real gut punch: if you ask that same girl at the age of sixteen, "Where's God?" there is a high probability that she'll respond with all sincerity, "I don't know if I believe in God." Be grateful that she says it, because by speaking the words she is asking for meaningful conversation. Nonetheless, we need to ask ourselves what happened. How did this child we've loved and nurtured so dearly move from understanding that God dwells within us, around us, among us, and between us to doubting the very existence of God? What happened?

At the innocent age of four, we are open to mystery and possibility. We don't expect the Alpha and Omega to contort to the limitations of reason and rationality. Also, at that age we have yet to bite into the apple of individualism and arrogance. We are humble, trusting, and fully accepting that we are one with others. For this reason, Jesus holds up a small child and says, "Truly I tell you, unless you change and become like children, you will never enter the kingdom of heaven. Whoever becomes humble like this child is the greatest in the kingdom of heaven" (Matthew 18:3–4).

When children hit the age of reason around seven, we try to explain God to them in terms they can understand, which inevitably means we define and confine the undefinable and unconfinable. We end up reducing this wondrous, infinite mystery of unitive oneness and omnipotent love to an image of an old guy-in-the-sky who, like Santa Claus, rewards us for good behaviors and punishes us for bad behaviors. For the most part, this works with first graders, but by the time kids hit high school, it doesn't add up anymore. They are searching for answers to big questions, seeking spiritual depth, and we respond by spoon-feeding rudimentary platitudes. Then we scratch our heads in bewilderment when they stop believing.

## The Class

Shortly after I was ordained, I was asked to serve as a substitute for one of my parish's confirmation classes. I find the challenging curiosity of high schoolers to be open and compelling, so I readily agreed. I was given a lesson plan to follow, but since all roads lead to God if you journey with a pilgrim's heart, I decided to walk with the students down whatever path they wanted to travel, much to the chagrin of Directors of Religious Education everywhere.

We sat in a circle, myself and seven high school juniors, and after greetings, pleasantries, and a short prayer, I opened it up. "None of you are here to serve me. I am here to serve you. So, the way I see it, this is your time, not mine. We have some material we're supposed to cover, and maybe we'll get to it, but first let's hear what you want to talk about. What's on your mind?"

Silence. Crickets. Of course there was silence. These were teenagers and none of them wanted to be there. I knew it, and they knew it. None of them was going to give me the satisfaction or take the social risk of engaging, at least not right away. What they didn't anticipate was that I am very comfortable with silence. We sat a little longer, until I finally smiled and said, "Thank you for this gift. Silence is my favorite prayer form. It's like a small but much needed sabbath at the end of a hectic day. Take a few deep breaths and enjoy it."

The quiet continued another twenty seconds or so until someone finally asked, "What does it even mean to be a deacon?" We talked about that for just a bit until the inevitable follow-up landed. "Why would you do that?" So, we had a little conversation about God's call and our response, about living with a sense of purpose and vocation. Then they wanted to get personal, so someone asked emphatically, "But why do *you* do it? Don't you have enough going on? Like, you have kids, right? And a job? Why did *you* want to be a deacon?"

I let out a long exhale. "I don't know," I confessed. "I felt spiritually called and knew I'd never find peace unless I followed that path. You're asking a rational question, and you want a rational answer. That makes sense, I suppose. But for me there is nothing rational about becoming a deacon. It is spiritual. I don't fully understand why I was called or what is expected of me, and I often feel like a fish out of water. I guess I had to decide whether I'd guide my life by logic or by faith, and I chose faith. Well, I chose both, actually, but at the end of the day, sometimes you just have to take a leap of faith."

And then it came. A young woman named Gretchen who had been intentionally aloof and noticeably disengaged rolled her eyes and muttered, "Oh, please."

## Gretchen

Normally, I love it when teens voice their doubts. It means they're engaged and thinking, and they're no longer willing to accept the puree fed to them as small children. They want something they can sink their teeth into and chew on. They're ready to venture deeper into truth, and they're holding the religion they've inherited accountable. This is good. They're sharp enough to know that truth should be able to stand up to challenge and objection. Also, they say out loud what many adults wonder but are afraid to put into words. But Gretchen wasn't looking for conversation or exploration; she was itching for a fight.

"This is all such BS," she said. "Religion is BS. People start wars because of religion. They kill each other in the name of a god that doesn't exist." Gretchen wasn't just rebellious; she was smart. And she was prepared. Before I could respond, she listed a litany of wars fought, suffering caused, and injustices perpetrated in the name of religions, saving her sharpest rebukes for Christianity in general and Catholicism in particular. And then, in front of the entire group, she put me on trial. "Throughout history, people have created and manipulated whatever theology they need to give moral justification to atrocities. How can you even defend religion?" she asked accusingly.

Eyes shifted from her to me. In that moment, I became poignantly aware that I wasn't merely responding to her. I was responding for the benefit of everyone in that room. Six other seventeen-year-old kids needed a response they could believe in. I knew better than to argue with Gretchen. That's what she wanted, and she had rehearsed that fight in her head a hundred times. I was outmatched.

But I had also studied enough martial arts to know how to use an attacker's momentum against themselves. I nodded and leaned in, addressing the group. "Gretchen's not wrong, you know. People have done some atrocious things in the name of religion. It would be wrong to deny it or to downplay it. But people have also done some amazingly loving things in the name of the religions they profess. They've fed the hungry, cared for the sick, sheltered the homeless, and welcomed refugees. So, I ask, is religion the problem or is the way some people misuse religion the problem?"

Gretchen was no slouch. She quickly retorted, "Everything you mentioned that is good, people could do all of it without religion."

"Yes," I agreed. "That's true. Absolutely. And everything evil that you mentioned people have done without religion. It sounds like you and I agree that religion is not the problem."

"OK," she conceded. "So why bother? What's the point of religion?"

"There it is!" I exclaimed. "A brilliant question. Now we have a topic for good conversation."

## The Atheist Enters

Gretchen intended to be a stone thrower. She certainly did not want to get down on her knees and draw in the dirt with Jesus. So, while the rest of the class sorted out the difference between religion as a code of conduct and religion as a roadmap leading toward ever-deepening spirituality, she sat and stewed a bit, calculating her next attack.

Let me pause for a moment and clarify that I really liked and appreciated Gretchen. She was honest and authentic, even if she was packing an agenda. From my perspective, she was outwardly representing a doubting voice that finds fertile ground in the recesses of most people's minds at some point, including the most faithful among us. I was grateful she brought it out of the whispered shadows and threw it on the table where we were forced to deal with it, even if it was challenging and uncomfortable.

When she was locked and loaded, she returned to the conversation. "Look," she blurted, "I am an atheist. The whole idea of God is ridiculous, so this whole conversation about getting closer to God is stupid."

You could feel the air leave the room. The other members of the group were exasperated, but ignoring the comment would give it power and arguing would give it legitimacy. Also, a yes/no debate about the existence of God is largely just another form of dualism. If we accept the identity of God in Exodus as *I AM* and in Revelation as *the Alpha and Omega*, then arguing about the existence of God is really an argument about existence, period. As the French philosopher and mathematician René Descartes famously concluded when he set out to prove the existence of God, "I think, therefore I am." The awareness of my own existence proves the existence of God. I am that I AM.

"What does that mean?" I asked. "When you say you don't believe in God, what exactly is it that you don't believe in?"

Gretchen was not prepared for that question. "The, um, I guess the whole idea," she stumbled. "I don't believe there is some sort of supreme being pulling all the strings."

"OK," I affirmed. "Fair enough. You don't believe in the idea of God that was presented to you as a small child. Neither do I. You don't believe God is a being who sits on a throne above the clouds granting some wishes and denying others." She nodded. "Neither do I," I added.

## The Believer Emerges

Gretchen had intended to pick a fight, and the one thing she was not prepared for was agreement. But I was determined to hold the room on common ground. I knew a little about Gretchen's backstory, that her father had passed away after a tough battle with cancer ten years earlier when she was in the first grade. She and her mom were very close, and she had no other family in the area. As far as I was concerned, she had every right to doubt the existence of God. It would be more surprising perhaps if she didn't.

"May I ask you something, Gretchen?"

She nodded consent.

"Do you believe in love?"

"What do you mean?" she asked. She tilted her head slightly and looked at me with authentic engagement, not with antagonism. For the first time, she was participating in the conversation openly and accepting me as someone other than an opponent.

"Well, you love your mom, right?" Again, she nodded, so I continued, "And that love is mutual. Your mom loves you as well?"

"Of course," she said, waving her hand with a gesture asking "Where is this going?"

"And that love is steadfast? You can count on it no matter what? You experience that love and you have faith in it?" Once she registered agreement, I brought it home. "Then I hate to break it to you, Gretchen, but our Catholic faith teaches that God is love. In the New Testament, St. John writes that God is love. If you experience love and you believe in that love, you are not an atheist. In fact, you have a deep and profound understanding of faith, and you believe in the same God I believe in."

I probably should not have said that last part. There is no level on which Gretchen wanted to be like me.

## The Conflict with Notions

Although she didn't realize it at the time, Gretchen wasn't denying the existence of God; she was rejecting a notion about God. She simply hadn't been introduced to a deeper, more expansive, more spiritually mature understanding. In my experience, the conflicts we have with God are almost always conflicts with our own human ideas about God.

There is a good reason why the ancient Hebrews refused to utter the name of God and went so far as to make God's name unpronounceable. As soon as we define who or what God is, we inherently draw lines that also define what God is not. The brilliance of Trinity is that it identifies God as all-inclusive of everything. God is the unifying Oneness of all creation and imagination. God is also the unifying Oneness of flesh and blood, of human experience, of self-giving love, and of the great mystery of birth, life, death, and resurrection. And God is the unifying Oneness of inspiration and awe, of courage and fortitude, and of wisdom and understanding. In other words, God is not *a* being, but rather *Being*, the great I AM, the Alpha and Omega.

We have conflicts with God because we tend to shrink God into a box small enough for us to understand. This enables us to assign our own human attributes and even character flaws to God. Thus, we manipulate God to serve our agendas, asking for mercy and expecting forgiveness for our transgressions, but judging others and expecting eternal retribution for their transgressions. And then, after taming and domesticating God so we can be in control, we pass the box to others and say, "Here. You need to believe in this, or you will go to hell." People with minds and discerning thought will of course reject this entire paradigm, and in doing so often will reject the very idea of God. Again, though, what they are refusing to accept is not the reality of God as Being, as Alpha and Omega, as unitive Oneness, and as love; rather, they are rejecting a notion of God as a controlling, punitive, sometimes petty puppet master.

## Reconciling with God

Becoming whole in our relationship with God takes work on our part: a lifetime of work. It requires an ever-deepening spiritual practice of letting go, specifically of letting go of ego, individualism, fear, insecurity, and all the other walls we build around our own hearts. It demands that we intentionally break down the barriers that hold us back, freeing ourselves to expand and grow into the universal Oneness of God. And it requires the vulnerability of openness, allowing the love we call God to permeate us entirely and flow into and through us.

On my desk is a sign given to me by my friend and mentor, Fr. Paul Demuth, which simply states the Benedictine value "Prayer & Work." Fr. Paul gave it to me in acknowledgment of the influence the Benedictine community of St. John's University in Collegeville, Minnesota, has had on my own spiritual journey. When I was first introduced to "Prayer & Work" many years ago, I saw them as two distinct things, reminding me of the two priorities in the spiritual life. Since then, I have grown to see them as partnering strands in a helix spiral, like DNA. In fact, I see them as the DNA of wholeness with God. My prayer is an ever-present awareness of God's immediate presence within me and around me. Some might call this the contemplative's path. And my work is the outflowing of that same unitive, loving presence. This is God coming to me, stirring within me, and flowing into the world through me—loving Creator upon me, loving flesh and blood within me, loving spirit flowing through me—the Father, Son, and Holy Spirit. Trinity.

part four

# Fusion vs. Friction

13

# The Gift of Tension

My friend Meg is five foot one when she's wearing heels. Her husband Marc is on the north side of six foot six. (He doesn't wear heels.) Marc grew up in Chicago and is passionate about the Bears. Meg was raised to be an avid Green Bay Packers fan, so much so that she has a green heart with a gold number 15 tattooed on her ankle. It's there to declare her lifelong devotion to the Packers' Hall of Fame quarterback and all-around great humanitarian, Bart Starr. She doesn't have a tattoo declaring her love for Marc. He says this doesn't bother him.

For the unfamiliar, the Packers–Bears rivalry has Hatfield–McCoy intensity. Yet, Meg and Marc remain happily married. What's more, Meg is a high-energy extrovert who is connected and involved at all times, whereas Marc is an introvert who quietly and contentedly retreats to his garage to work on cars. On Friday nights after an exhausting week, Meg wants to unwind by going out and spending time among happy people, but Marc prefers to stay home and watch a movie. Also, he's Catholic and she is "a lot of things," to use her words. They recently celebrated twenty-nine years of wedded bliss, and I don't know of any couple who is a better fit for each other.

Early in their relationship, Marc and Meg promised each other they would use their differences to create wholeness, like the north and south poles of a magnet. It provided them with context to not only accept but to respect and embrace the unique character of each other.

## Tension Is Life

It is the nature of the human condition to live in tension. Male and female, light and dark, self-preservation and self-sacrifice, joy and sorrow, life and death. Anyone who has ever lived with teenagers knows that tension is both inevitable and uncomfortable. Dependence and independence, structure and fluidity, rules and rebellion.

We get in trouble because we try to resolve tension rather than reconcile it. How many of us have said to our teenage children, "As long as you live under my roof, you will follow my rules." We like to call this *tough love*—and maybe there are times when it is—but mostly it's an attempt to resolve the tension through power. The resolution is simple: my way or the highway. But this approach can put boundaries on love, coercing young people to conform to the way we want them to be rather than encouraging them to grow into the person God created them to be. I know fathers who destroyed their relationships with their sons due to arguments over hair length or ear piercings. Ultimately, through the power of parenthood, these men got the resolution they wanted, but years later they remain a long way from reconciliation with their sons.

Meg and Marc chose a different path for their relationship. They reconcile the tension by using it to create wholeness rather than division. Packers and Bears, extroversion and introversion—there is room in their love for all the above. As mentioned earlier, resolution often leaves brokenness, but reconciliation restores wholeness.

## Holding Tension

Many years ago, I happened upon a study that completely changed my approach to parenthood, marriage, leadership, and all relationships. A couple of Harvard professors set out to identify the personality characteristics that effective leaders have in common. They identified several dozen CEOs from top-performing companies and interviewed each in depth. As it turns out, they have nothing in common, no universal traits or patterns that predicate success—except for one thing: they all demonstrated an ability to hold tension. They were perfectly comfortable allowing two seemingly opposed ideas to both be true, and they merely held the tension without needing to resolve it.

I decided to work on incorporating that same ethos in my own life. What I've learned is that when we try to resolve tension, we end up creating friction. Earlier, I discussed the brokenness inherent in the conservative/liberal paradigm. The need for one side to be right and the other to be wrong has created untold social and political friction. It has destroyed marriages and divided families. But once we accept that the paradigm is a false and artificial construct, we open ourselves to fusion rather than friction. We have the option to hold the tension and allow both things to be true. Both the

Packers and the Bears can be worthy of passionate loyalty. (It hurt me a little to admit that.) We really can be responsible stewards of the environment and advance economic prosperity. We can have secure borders and welcome refugees. We can teach our children to both respect familial cooperation and honor who they authentically are. The notion that tension must be divisive and cannot be unitive is an offense to spiritual imagination.

## Fusion as Natural Reconciliation

The sun, which makes life on earth possible, is a fusion reactor. Electromagnetism, the force pulsing the positive and negative charges that power everything from our heartbeats to supercomputers, is a fusion dynamic. The reproduction of life, with two cells converging, is a fusion process. All life depends on seemingly opposite things coming together in unity. Alpha and Omega, the beginning and the end.

Fusion, not friction, is the life force of the universe. This is how the Creator makes all things whole and harmonious. If we are truly sincere about living in wholeness and harmony ourselves, united with Creator and creation in sacred Oneness, we will seek to align our own hearts, minds, and souls with fusion.

14

# Me vs. We: Individualism and Universalism

Coach Chuck called his team back to the sidelines. The opposing team was already in position, ready to start the second half, when his voice reverberated across the pitch. "Everyone get back over here! Now!" Eleven twelve-year-old young men in blue shirts turned around and walked confusingly back toward their coach. The eyes and ears of four dozen parents and grandparents followed them with confusion.

Chuck had had enough. He hadn't intended to coach a team that summer. Instead, he planned to sit in a lawn chair off to the side and just enjoy watching his son play soccer. Besides, he had explained to his wife, their son was at an age where he would benefit from the influence of other male role models.

Unfortunately, the team's original coach brought a win-at-all-costs style that was praised by some parents and reviled by others. There were phone calls, letters of complaint, and difficult meetings. The board ultimately decided his approach to the game was not compatible with the spirit of the league. He had to go, and they called Chuck. It was already two weeks into the season, and either Chuck would step in, or the team would be dissolved.

So, there he was, suddenly coaching a team of young men he didn't know. One third came from families that resented the dismissal of the previous coach, one third from families who were grateful, and the final third were just confused by the whole mess. Chuck really didn't want to be a part of any of it. Still, there was a need, and he had the experience and skillset to address it, so he stepped up.

## There Is No "I" in Team, But Apparently There Is a "Me"

The first thing Chuck noticed when he took over the team was that this group of boys had no sense of comradery. They came from five different schools and barely knew one another's names. Most notably, they lacked any semblance of playing as a single unit. They were just a group of fourteen individuals all wearing the same-color shirts. So, Chuck moved them around and had them play positions they hadn't played before, alongside teammates they never even talked to. It didn't go well. In the first game, they were beaten handily by a below-average opponent.

The first half of the second game didn't go any better, and they were down 2–0. Chuck talked to the guys about putting themselves into position to help each other out, about creating passing lanes and drawing defenders to open space for teammates. It was all foundational soccer stuff. He concluded with his oft-repeated message: "What you do when you don't have the ball, when no one is paying attention to you, is more important than what you do when you have the ball." Then he gave them their assignments and sent them onto the pitch for the second half.

As they slowly walked away, Chuck could hear the grumbling.

"I don't want to play midfield."

"Defense? I should be a striker."

"I hate playing on the right side."

And that's when Coach Chuck called them all back to the sidelines.

**The Speech**

I think you could call it a speech. Some might call it a lecture. One could even argue it was a sermon. My father would have called it an ass-chewing. Maybe it was all of the above. When the boys arrived back at the sideline, Coach Chuck had them sit on the grass while he unloaded.

"I heard you," he said. "Everyone heard you. We all heard you whine and complain about your position assignments. I'll get to that in a sec."

The referee called over, "Coach, we need your team on the field."

Chuck put his hand up and called back loud enough for everyone in the park to hear, "Hang on, sir. We're doing something here that's more important than this game. Give us a minute, please." That's when everyone went silent and strained to hear. After all, what could possibly be more important than a youth soccer match?

Turning back to his team, Chuck was fully aware that he was now talking to at least sixty people. "There are fourteen members of this team. I want each of you to look at the other thirteen. Don't look at me. Don't look at the ground. Look at each other." They hesitated so Chuck got animated. "Do it! Look at each other right now or you'll never play another minute on this team! Look each other in the eye!" Heads snapped up and fourteen twelve-year-old boys did something they hadn't done before. They noticed each other and saw reflections of themselves. Coach Chuck continued, "Do you think all your teammates came out here today to make sure *you* get to do what *you* want? Do you think they're all here to serve *you*? Now look over at that other team. Look at the referees. Look around at all these people sitting in lawn chairs. Do you honestly think that all these people came out here today to make sure *you* get to do what *you* want?" He paused just long enough to let that soak in. "Now look at yourself. I'm not talking about soccer here. I'm talking about who you are as a human being, about who you intend to be as a man. Are you going to go through life like this, expecting the world and everyone in it to make sure *you* get what *you* want, and then snivel and whine when it doesn't work out that way? Or are you going to grow into the sort of man who puts the *we* before the *me* in life? Are you going to serve something greater than yourself, or are you going to expect everyone else to serve the greatness of the almighty you? Think about it, but you don't have long. As you grow through your teen years, you will each become more of who you already are. So, who are you? Are you a self-absorbed little boy who whines when he doesn't get what he wants? Or are you a young man who is ready to step up and serve something bigger than self? If you want to be the star of your own show, then put on a skirt and go play tennis and it can be all about you. But if you want to play this sport and be a part of this team, then you better cowboy up right now and decide to serve each other. Because this doesn't all revolve around you. The world doesn't revolve around you. Life doesn't revolve around you. Got it? Great people raise up others, not themselves. Now run back out on that pitch and show me, show your teammates, show everyone else, but most importantly show yourself who you are as a human being!"

**Zach's Parents**

Although trying to remain poised on the outside, Chuck was quaking on the inside. He had raised his voice and yelled at the kids publicly, in front of God and everyone. He knew that the comment about putting on a skirt and playing tennis wasn't really appropriate and could get him in a lot of trouble. He probably ticked off a few parents with that one. Trying to focus, he took a few deep breaths. The conversation in his head was racing. "Let them come for me. I don't care. I mean, they wouldn't be wrong if they did, but I do not care. The boys needed to hear it. I didn't ask for any of this. Get your head straight, Chuck. Focus on the game. You can deal with the fallout later."

Out of the corner of his eye, he saw two parents walking toward him. "Not here. Not now. I'm in no mood," he thought to himself. He took a few steps toward the field and pretended not to notice them. "One word," he thought, "if they say one word about what just happened, I will hand them this clipboard and whistle and walk away. They can coach. I'll go sit in their chairs." He glanced and saw them getting close, too close to ignore, so he turned to square up with them.

"Hi, Coach," they said extending their hands. "We're Zach's parents. We just wanted to come over and thank you for the gift you just gave our son." Chuck was floored. He had not expected that. "We heard every word," Zach's mom said. "I wish I had recorded it so I could play it back to him every day until he leaves for college." Then Zach's dad picked up the dialog, "Zach really needed to hear what you just said from someone who isn't me. He's at an age where he's starting to think he knows more than his dad, so I am grateful that you said what you said. Listen," he continued, "you got thrown into an impossible situation here. Thank you for doing it. Don't worry about any of the other parents. We'll handle them. Just keep doing what you just did."

## The We Before the Me

At the core of the challenge Chuck levied upon his team was the question of whether they would be the type of people who put the *we* before the *me* in life. The question was asked in the context of a team sport, but it wasn't about the team or the sport. It was and is about who we serve as human beings. Do we live to serve self, or do we live to serve the greater good of God's creation?

Another way of asking this question about the orientation of our hearts, minds, and souls is this: Are we living as individualists or as universalists? Are we seeking to live apart as one, or as part of One?

Christianity in general and Catholicism in particular profess this, but I am not convinced the message comes through. As expanded on earlier, it is central to incarnation, Eucharist, and resurrection, but I wonder if we leave it there and don't walk away with a contrary message.

Many among the religiously devout, including several priests and even some bishops, have told me over the years that the whole purpose of life is to get to heaven. To be clear, those are their exact words: *to get to heaven*. I could accept that if the understanding of heaven being advanced was the complete unification in Oneness with Creator and creation. But this isn't what they seem to mean. Instead, devoutly religious voices continue to perpetuate the rudimentary, and dare I suggest juvenile, notion that heaven is a reward for good behavior.

If there is any hope for wholeness and reconciliation here, now, and forever after, we will need to open ourselves to a more profound and significantly more enriching and rewarding reality.

When Jesus was asked to name the greatest commandment, he did not say, "To get to heaven." Instead, he said, "'You shall love the Lord your God with all your heart, and with all your soul, and with all your mind.' This is the greatest and first commandment. And a second is like it: 'You shall love your neighbor as yourself'" (Matthew 22:37–39). If you want to argue that this is indeed what heaven is, then, my friend, we are of One mind.

Peace be with you.